COCONUT CUISINE

featuring Stevia

D0000881

Jan London

Book Publishing Company
Summertown, Tennessee

Jan London can be contacted through www.happystomach.com.

Printed in the U.S. by
Book Publishing Company
P.O. Box 99
Summertown, TN 38483
www.bookpubco.com
888-260-8458

16 15 14 13 12 11 10 09 08 07 06   1 2 3 4 5 6 7 8 9

ISBN 10 1-57067-196-6
ISBN 13 978-1-57067-196-8

Library of Congress Cataloging-in-Publication Data
London, Jan, 1946-
    Coconut cuisine : featuring stevia / Jan London.
        p. cm.
    Includes index.
    ISBN-13: 978-1-57067-196-8
    ISBN-10: 1-57067-196-6
    1. Cookery (Coconut) 2. Cookery (Stevia)   I. Title.
    TX814.2.C63L66 2006
    641.6'461--dc22   2006010341

Disclaimer
The advice offered in this book is based upon the author's own experience and
is not intended to replace a qualified healthcare professional. The author shall
have neither liability nor responsibility to any person or entity that incurs any
loss, damage or injury caused directly, or indirectly from information provided in
this book.

Printed in the U.S. on 100% recycla-
ble natural wood fiber from U.S.
forests. The lay-flat binding allows
pages to open flat for easier reading.

The nutritional calculations included
with each recipe are all based on a
2,000 calorie diet. Only those vitamin
and minerals that exceed a 25% daily
value are listed.

Table of Contents

Introduction

Like most everyone else, I was raised on the Standard American Diet. In mid-century America, there was no information, no warnings about the harmful effects of hydrogenated oils, processed sugar, sodium chloride or pesticides. In fact, food was hardly attributed to illness.

Then, in the early seventies, the shift toward more conscious food choices began and I eagerly followed. As my diet gradually changed toward more plant-based foods, my attitude and my health began to improve and my life took another direction. My passion to learn more about the healing nature of foods led me to the Far East and to Europe where I lived for twelve years. I studied macrobiotic cooking in harmony with Taoist principles under the guidance of my mentor, Mayli. I express these insightful teachings through my cooking, which I hope will inspire other seekers of health and lovers of great cuisine.

This cookbook has been created through a natural progression of my love for coconut and stevia herb that began in Sri Lanka, 1983. During that year, my diet was comprised primarily of coconut. Its sweet water satisfied my thirst and gave me energy; its flesh added wonderful flavor to sauces; its oil nourished my body inside and out. I clearly recognized it as a food of the gods.

Shortly after I returned to the US in 1995, my sister introduced me to stevia lemonade. I loved it. As I began to experiment with stevia's different forms in a wide range of dishes, I recognized its potential as the sweet flavor to replace high calorie grain and fruit sweeteners.

When the truth about coconut's healing properties was exposed and good quality coconut oil became available, providence ensued and *Coconut Cuisine featuring Stevia* was born.

I have provided a broad range of information on coconuts and stevia in the following chapters to illustrate the profound effects they can contribute to our lives.

Happy stomach!

All About Coconuts

"One of these nuts is a meal for a man, both meat and drink."
Marco Polo

"He who plants a coconut tree plants food and drink, vessels
and clothing, a home for himself and a heritage for his
children." - South Seas saying

The coconut palm is one of the oldest trees on the planet
and has existed since the age of the dinosaurs. It flourish-
es in tropical climates from Southeast Asia to Polynesia,
India, the Pacific Islands, Hawaii, South America, the
Caribbean and in South Florida.

Revered as the most useful tree on earth, the coconut
palm has generously provided civilizations with all their
needs to survive. Its roots, fronds and trunk are used for
shelter, light, furniture and household utensils. But its
most sacred part is its fruit, the coconut. A hard outer
green shell protects its precious nut-like seed that is
covered in a hairy brown husk. This husk provides fuel for
cooking, fiber for clothing and a rope, which is stronger
than hemp. Within this seed lies the true essence of the
coconut palm – its water, meat and oil - its life giving
force.

During the months that this seed matures, it goes through
two major stages: first the young coconut, with its soft,
jelly-like meat and sweet revitalizing water that quenches
thirst and provides energy; the second and most potent
stage produces the mature nut. After harvesting the nut
and removing the water, workers shell the nuts by hand.
The inner skin, a thin brown layer, is cut away leaving
pure thick, white coconut meat. Milk, cream and oil are
extracted from this meat. The milk and cream are used for
the ubiquitous curry sauces and desserts, and the oil is
used for cooking, body massage, to nourish the skin, nails
and hair and applied topically on wounds to speed healing.

The coconut has always been prized for its medicinal qualities. Yet, it also has the reputation as an aphrodisiac because of its ability to stimulate the production of hormones in both the male and female. When used as body oil and blended with stimulating spices such as cayenne pepper, it acts as a carrier to circulate the blood and to stimulate the organs, while its aromatic scent enhances the senses. The highly mineral-charged water acts to detoxify the kidneys, which indirectly affects its neighbors, the reproductive organs. Healthy kidneys are believed to promote a vibrant, healthy attitude, which expresses itself through the normal, healthy desire for sexual and emotional fulfillment. In a greater sense, this cycle is the silent call of nature to preserve the species. The coconut also has a symbolic meaning. Its very shape, with its three holes and long protective fibers, is compared to the human head and face, representing its importance as a basic food for mankind. Moreover, these three openings form a triangle, which represent the yin yang symbol of ancient religions.

After years of research, western medicine has just recently confirmed the profound healing properties of coconut, dispelling decades of misleading information. According to the results of these findings, coconut's form of saturated fat actually helps prevent heart disease, stroke and hardening of the arteries. Unlike other oils and fats, coconut oil contains a large amount of the fatty acid known as lauric acid, which is the predominant fatty acid found in mother's milk. The lauric acid makes breast milk easily digestible, it strengthens the immune system and protects against viral, bacterial and fungal infections. Studies have shown coconut oil's effectiveness with HIV, SARS, Crohn's Disease, as well as other chronic illnesses. It detoxifies the liver, helps to build lipoproteins, fats and hormones and bile, which is necessary for digestion. Coconut's amazing healing properties are also attributed to reducing the risk of other degenerative conditions such as cancer, osteoporosis, and diabetes. The medium chain fatty acids help to create a healthy digestive tract, which in turn allows for better digestion and absorption of the nutrients in our foods. They also speed up metabolism providing an immediate source of energy while supplying fewer calories than other fats. It is the oil of choice for dieters and for hypothyroidism. Coconut oil helps protect against skin cancer and other blemishes and helps prevent premature aging and wrinkling. As a cooking oil, it is highly resistant to heat and spoilage. In fact, coconut oil has been called "the healthiest dietary oil on earth".

Most coconut oil sold in America is refined. The excessive heat, bleaching and chemical solvents used in the refining process creates a thick, yellowish-white product that is tasteless and odorless. Only the organic, extra virgin, expeller or hand pressed coconut oil retains its white color, light texture, and its mild taste and scent of fresh coconut.

Coconut oil is truly an ideal food: It is not hydrogenated, contains no trans fats and is very stable with a long shelf life. It is a wonderful substitute for butter or margarine and because it does not revert to trans fatty acids when heated, it is a healthy choice for cooking.

Coconut products used in my recipes include:

Coconut Oil - Organic, unrefined, extra virgin, hand or cold-pressed is the most superior quality and the best tasting.

Coconut water - Packaged directly from the young coconut, its sweet taste satisfies thirst and sweet cravings and contains no fat. It provides the alkaline balance to an acidic condition, which is the primary cause of most illnesses. Coconut water works on a cellular level. It contains the most concentrated amounts of cytokinins than any other food source. These are the cell's DNA protective agents. When cytokinins are present, the cells can then replicate to form a perfect copy of its DNA. If they are not present, imperfect cells are formed resulting in future chronic illnesses.

Coconut Milk - This is a blend of coconut water and coconut cream resulting in a wonderful milk emulsion, containing 17 % fat. A word of caution: Look for canned coconut milk that does not contain some kind of binder, such as carrageen.

Coconut Cream - This is pressed out of the meat of the mature coconut. Compared to the coconut milk, it is higher in oil and in the healthy medium chain fatty acids, containing 22% fat. It is similar in taste, although not as sweet with a rich, thick texture making it ideal for pudding recipes.

Coconut Spread - It is made by grinding the dried flesh of mature coconuts. Because the meat of the coconut is so high in oils, the result is a delicious thick paste very similar to sesame tahini, and it is shelf stable. This spread contains over 60% medium chain fatty acids known for their antibacterial, antiviral, antiparasitical and energy giving properties.

Coconut Flakes - Not all coconut flake products are the same. Most air-dried shredded and flaked coconut products found in conventional supermarkets have a weak coconut taste and contain additives such as propylene glycol, sugar and sulfites to preserve it. Always check the ingredients on the label even from health food stores. Freeze dried coconut flakes have a very sweet taste and contain no preservatives or chemical additives. They are freshly frozen to 20 degrees F below zero and then dried, retaining the nutrients.

I have used Wilderness Family Naturals' coconut products in my recipes.

In some countries, coconuts are gathered by trained monkeys.

All About Stevia

Stevia is nature's sweet gift to all of us. This remarkable plant, from the rainforests of Paraguay, is up to 300 times sweeter than sugar, does not affect blood sugar levels, and has no calories. It is nutritious, noncarcenogenic, nontoxic, and safe for diabetics and hypoglycemics.

Stevia leaves have been used for 1500 years by the Guarani Indians of Paraguay as a soothing tonic for the stomach and as a healing concentrate when cooked in water. It was first discovered and introduced to Europe in 1899 by M. S. Bertoni. Since then, hundreds of scientific tests have been performed on these sweet leaves, which have been found to contain, among other elements, Vitamin C, calcium, beta-carotene, chromium, fiber, iron, magnesium, niacin, potassium, protein and silicon. It is the intensely sweet glycosides, referred to as steviosides, produced within the leaves, which make stevia so sweet. Research has shown that the body does not digest or metabolize these intensely sweet glycosides. They are not converted into glucose in the body and, therefore, have a glycemic index of 0. This makes stevia a most valuable sweetening source for those with sugar restrictions, such as diabetes, hypoglycemia, or weight control.

Today, stevioside has a 52% share of the commercial sweetener market in Japan and is rapidly becoming the favored sweetener in China and throughout the Orient. In fact, China has become the major grower and processor of the stevia plant. Most stevia farmers cultivate their plants without the use of pesticides and under the conditions required for organic certification.

Additional Information:

Presently, the FDA will only allow stevia products to be distributed as a dietary supplement. Despite sweeping toxicology tests and widespread global use without incidence of adverse reaction, stevia has yet to be approved as a food source by the FDA. They rejected two comprehensive petitions submitted in the 1990's citing insufficient proof of stevia's safety. Consequently, because of this ruling, stevia is sold only in the nutritional supplement section in health food stores. Paradoxically, the FDA-approved sweetener, aspartame, receives one of the highest number of consumer complaints made to the FDA.

For the last several years, many Japanese farmers have been growing their fruits and vegetables with a powerful and effective fertilizer formulated from the leaves and stems of the stevia plant. These crops are noticeably tastier, more fragrant, have a higher sugar and nutrient value and remain fresher longer. Additionally, this plant food also prevents and cures plant diseases, dissolves agrochemicals in the soil, increases their harvest, and makes the plants more resistant to frost and strong winds. When used with other composting materials such as manure and kitchen refuse, it greatly accelerates fermentation without noxious fumes, producing high-quality organic manure in less than 3 months. A formula produced for fisheries, livestock and for humans has also reported amazing results.

Health Benefits of Stevia

It is estimated that over 500 scientific studies have been performed on stevia. Many scientists have reported numerous health benefits to adding stevia to the daily diet.

Scientific research indicates that stevia effectively regulates blood sugar in people with diabetes and hypoglycemia, bringing it in line with more normal levels. Studies have indicated that stevia tends to lower elevated blood pressure while not affecting people with normal blood pressure.

Stevia inhibits the growth and reproduction of oral bacteria and other infectious organisms. Regular users of stevia as a mouthwash or for brushing teeth (added to toothpaste) have reported an improvement to bleeding gum problems. This inhibition of oral bacteria may explain why users of stevia-enhanced products report a lower incidence of colds and flu. Subsequently, an increasing number of toothpaste manufacturers are now using stevia in their products.

When applied externally stevia poultices and extracts have been observed to have therapeutic effect on acne, seborrhea, dermatitis and eczema. Extracts placed directly in cuts and wounds, have demonstrated rapid healing without scarring.

Other benefits of adding stevia to the daily diet include improved digestion and soothed upset stomachs.

Stevia is also an exceptional aid in weight loss management because it contains no calories and reduces the craving for sweets and fatty foods. Steviosides, the principle sugar molecule component of stevia, pass through the human alimentary canal without being altered by digestive processes, demonstrating remarkable stability. They simply cannot be broken down into their metabolites under normal gastric conditions. As a result, the sugar molecules pass unchanged through the human gastrointestinal tract and are not absorbed into the blood, producing no calories. Preliminary research indicates that stevia may actually reset the hunger mechanism in people where the zpathway between the hypothalamus and the stomach has become obstructed. In other words, it clears the communication pathway between the stomach and the brain, reducing hunger sensations faster.

Stevia Products

Whole Leaf Stevia is simply the dried stevia leaf. It is available as tea bags and sold loose in cut and powder forms. Because of stevia's growing popularity, it is now being grown in the US. These plants can be ordered from local growers. The freshly cut leaves can be added to flavor soups, stews and hot or cold liquids, or boiled to make your own liquid extract.

Stevia Concentrate is prepared by cooking stevia leaves in water to produce a thick, dark liquid with a licorice taste. It blends well with aromatic spices and with dishes that are enhanced by this flavor. Because the foods it is blended with take on its color, it makes a good substitute for molasses or brown sugar. It can be used full strength as a facial mask or diluted in water as an effective mouth-wash. To relieve a sore throat, squirt a dropper full or more into the mouth and allow it to coat the affected area. Refrigerate after opening.

Stevia Extract is a white powder containing only the sweet glycoside molecules extracted from the stevia leaf. It is the most concentrated form of all stevia products, approximately 200 to 300 times sweeter than sugar. It does not lose its sweetness at high temperatures.

Stevia Clear Liquid is a blend of stevia extract powder and water. Alcohol or grapefruit seed extract is added as the necessary preservative. Refrigerate after opening.

Stevia Extract with Filler is the powdered extract form blended with a filler. These include: maltodextrin, derived from cornstarch; fructooligosaccharides—FOS, a plant-based fiber; and erythritol, derived from fruit.

Stevia extract, stevia clear liquid and stevia extract with filler are all interchangeable in my recipes. Only their strengths are different. I find it easier to blend the liquid form with liquid ingredients and the powder form with dry ingredients. Because stevia extract powder is 200 to 300 times sweeter than sugar, it is nearly impossible to give exact measurements for very small amounts. I describe this small quantity as a dusting in my recipes, which means to gently tap the container. Until you become familiar with its strength, one tap at a time, then taste tested for the result, will prevent overuse. Stevia clear liquid should also be used cautiously by adding a few drops at a time to attain the perfect sweetness for you. I describe this method as "to taste" in some of my recipes. Because of its user-friendly eyedropper, it is the easiest form to work with. Stevia extract with filler is considerably less sweet than the extract and liquid forms, and thus can be sprinkled more freely. Stevia concentrate and ground stevia leaf are the purest of all forms and have the most nutritional value.

Approximate Stevia Sweetness Equivalents:

1/3 to 1/2 tsp. extract powder	= 1 cup sugar
1 tsp. clear liquid	= 1 cup sugar
1 TBS stevia concentrate (water based)	= 1 cup sugar
1-1/2 to 2 TBS ground or cut stevia leaf	= 1 cup sugar
1-1/2 to 2 TBS stevia extract powder with filler	= 1 cup sugar
18 to 24 individual stevia packets	= 1 cup sugar
2 tsp. stevia concentrate (water based)	= 1 cup brown sugar

I have used SweetLeaf stevia products in my recipes.

Excerpts from the article, Living LaDolce Vida with Stevia, by Helen K. Chang, reprinted with permission of Total Health Magazine.

Quality of your Food

Choose your ingredients wisely, for they will determine the taste and nutritional value of your meal.

ORGANIC food has a superior quality and taste. The soil these fruits, vegetables, legumes and grains have been grown in is alive. Mass-produced fruits and vegetables grown on inorganic soil contain synthetic herbicides, pesticides and chemicals. This is increasingly linked to birth defects, cancer and other problems. This food lacks energy, nutritional value and most obviously, taste. Organic produce and products may cost more, but it is well worth it. If your local markets do not carry organic foods, you can purchase everything you need on the Internet.

SALT comes from the sea. However, not all salt is the same and this difference can either heal you or harm you.

Table salt, or sodium chloride, is a refined sea salt. Nearly all of its sixty trace minerals present in its natural state have been removed and replaced with dextrose, a sugar, to stabilize the added iodine, anti-caking chemicals, potassium iodide, and aluminum silicate. Aluminum is toxic and has been linked to one of the primary causes of Alzheimer's disease. Some serious health complications may arise without these essential minerals that have been removed. Magnesium is one of these. Without it, calcium cannot be absorbed into the body. Calcium is needed for strengthening bones, nerves, heart and muscles and for brain development. Without magnesium, the kidneys and gall bladder are affected, making them more susceptible to the formation of stones. An additional imbalance created by insufficient magnesium is an incessant craving for salt. Just a note on kidney stones: Kidney stones are comprised of calcium and oxalates. Foods highest in oxalates are red meats, rhubarb, Swiss chard, beet greens, and peanuts. As a preventative measure for kidney stones, eat high fiber grains and vegetables and avoid table salt like the plague.

Refined sea salt has a fine, white grain. Essential minerals have also been refined out. Beware that most of the sea salt that is sold is this highly refined variety.

Unprocessed sea salt has a grayish color and is slightly damp. It is vital to our health, if not overused. It contains many essential minerals and trace elements, which are very similar to that of our blood. Its alkalizing quality helps to balance an acidic condition as well as acid-forming foods such as meats, legumes, fruits and grains, and allows the body to easily digest them. Biologists claim that in order for us to maintain a healthy immune system, we must regularly replenish the naturally occurring trace elements in unprocessed sea salt.

Eating too much or not enough salt will cause health problems. The right amount is different for each individual, while the following remains a constant:

- Use natural sea salt cooked into the foods, not added at the table.
- In cooking, salt should not dominate the taste of food. Use it to bring out the food's natural sweetness.
- Most canned, packaged and prepared foods contain too much salt.
- Read labels.

CARBOHYDRATES are greatly misunderstood. Popularly alluded to as 'carbs', they all have acquired the reputation for making us fat. However, there are significant differences between them.
There are two types of carbohydrates – simple and complex. Both exist in either a natural or refined form. The refined forms of both are processed foods. These contain refined sugars and few essential vitamins and minerals

needed to maintain health and energy levels. Examples of the simple form include sugar, fruit juices, and refined molasses and honey. They digest quickly, causing an immediate high followed by depression. Complex refined forms include baked goods, refined pasta, breakfast cereals and pizza. Furthermore, eating too much of either of these refined forms can cause food cravings. These are the 'carbs' that should be avoided.

Natural Form of Carbohydrates

Simple carbohydrates - Your best choices are from seasonal fruit. Although these also digest quickly and cause the same reaction as the refined form, they contain essential vitamins and minerals. In their natural state, fruits quench thirst and have a cooling effect on hot summer days. Cooking seasonal fruit with a pinch of sea salt in cold weather adds a warming quality, produces a sweeter flavor and is more digestible.

Complex carbohydrates take longer to digest providing the energy for our daily activity and contain fiber, vitamins and minerals. Most experts recommend that 50 to 60 per cent of the total calories in our diet should come from complex carbohydrates in the form of whole grains, legumes, vegetables, whole grain breads and whole grain pasta.

To obtain the most benefit from whole grains, chew them very well. Digestion begins with this process. Saliva alkalizes the mildly forming acidity of these grains turning them into a form of sugar during their digestion. This natural form of sugar balances our metabolism slowly while appeasing our appetite. Adding a pinch of sea salt during their cooking process also helps to alkalize them.

When the elements of fire and time are added to root vegetables, long simmering carrots, onions, parsnips, and rutabaga become sugar-sweet, easier to digest and satisfy a sweet craving.

HEATING ELEMENTS

Fire is a life force that gives energy and vitality to the food and results in a more superior taste. Cooking on wood burning and natural gas stoves are also more efficient as they allow the flame to be easily adjusted for accurate cooking temperatures.

Electric cooking changes the molecular structure of the food, which strongly effects our nourishment and digestion. Temperature settings are slow to react which can result in over cooked or burnt food. Radiant style stove tops cook the food at an even higher vibration than electric cooking. In both cases, the flavor of the food is compromised.

Microwave heating uses an electromagnetic microwave generator tuned to a very high vibrational frequency. Its effect destroys from 60% to 90% of the vital energy field in foods. Life force moves in a spiral, clockwise direction, while microwaves move in a counter clockwise direction. This opposite force creates friction, which heats the food. This counter force, which breaks down life's energy, has serious consequences.

Research has shown that microwave ovens convert substances cooked in it to dangerous carcinogenic products and causes abnormal changes in human blood and immune systems. Also the nutritive value of B-complex vitamins, Vitamin C, Vitamin E and essential minerals in all foods is significantly decreased. Still, the most obvious consequence lies in the flavorless taste of the food. Just compare oven baked to micro-cooked. And its advantage as a time saver to stovetop cooking has been overstated. Actually, the stovetop does not take that much more time. Is this time you may save really worth the health risks?

Cooking Procedures

Experimenting with various cooking methods develops an intuitive instinct and a conscious approach. For example: long, slow cooking gives a soothing quality, sweeter taste and softer texure; fast and hot gives vitality.

Blanching - Blanching lightly cooks the vegetable, retaining its crispness and color. To blanch vegetables add them to boiling salted water for a short period of time, and then immediately place them in cold water until they cool. For other vegetables and fruits, such as tomatoes and peaches, a brief blanching loosens the skin while keeping the flesh firm, making them easier to peel. Do not add too many at one time or it will take longer to cook. Work in batches if necessary.

Wok Stir-Fry (Chinese Style) - In stir-frying, the food is always in motion. It cooks quickly over a high heat with a small amount of oil. Spread it around the pan or up the sides of the wok away from the center of the heat, then toss it together again in the center and repeat. This method keeps the vegetables crisp.

Place the wok on high heat. When it is hot, add oil. Wait a moment, then test the oil with a drop of water. If it sizzles it is hot enough. Do not allow the oil to smoke. Add aromatics such as garlic or ginger. In less than a minute they will begin to release their flavor, and you can begin to add the vegetables in order of their cooking times; those that take the longest are added first. Toss ingredients until they are evenly cooked without scorching; then add liquid ingredients and seasonings. For thinly sliced or shredded dishes, turn down the heat for a few minutes while flavors combine, adjust seasonings and serve. For dishes with larger cut ingredients, place a lid over the wok and adjust the temperature to maintain a simmer so that food steams until it has absorbed a portion or all of the liquid.

The basic pattern for many Chinese dishes is to pre-heat the pan or wok, add the oil and heat it, stir-fry the vegetables, add sauce and seasonings, thicken the sauce and serve.

Steaming - Fill water to at least one inch below the steamer. Place vegetables of the same texture and cut in the steamer. Keep the lid slightly opened to allow air in, retaining the color. Cook just until tender.

Water Sauté - Place 1/4 inch of spring water in a pot, add 1 TB olive oil, salt and minced garlic. Bring to a boil and add finely cut vegetables or chopped leafy greens. Cook, lid slightly opened, for 5 minutes or until crisp, yet tender.

Sauté - Start with thinly or small cut vegetables. Preheat the pan on medium to high heat, and then add a small amount of oil to cover the bottom of the pot or skillet. Turn heat to medium low. Add onions first to eliminate the smell. When they have turned translucent, they are done. Add white and green vegetables next, followed by orange and yellow. When adding new vegetables, place them in the middle closest to the heat and oil. Add a little sea salt to bring out their moisture. Allow them to cook in their own juices by leaving the lid on. Add just enough liquid to prevent scorching. Add more sea salt or tamari near the end of their cooking. The vegetables should be dry when finished.

Pressure Cook - Place ingredients, sea salt (omit if cooking legumes or winter squash) and required amount of spring water in the pot. Cook on high heat until the pressure comes up. Turn to low and cook for required time. Turn off the heat and allow the pressure to come down on its own for a more gentle result. Or, place the pot under cool running water until the pressure comes down. (Don't allow the water to run over the gauge).

Cutting Techniques

Cutting Techniques - There is one rule for all cutting techniques: each cut must be uniform to ensure even cooking and a pleasing presentation. To avoid cutting yourself, curl your fingers in using the blade as a guide, then use your fingertips to move the vegetable.

Diagonal - This can be cut to any thickness. When using scallions for garnish, slice thinly at a steep angle.

Matchsticks or Julienne - Start with the diagonal cut, sliced to the desired thickness. Then neatly stack 3 or 4 slices and slice through lengthwise in 3 or 4 equal cuts.

Half Moons - Cut vegetable in half lengthwise, and then cut across to desired thickness.

Dice or Mince - A dice is a small cube, larger than a mince. To dice an onion, first cut it in half from root to tip and peel it. Lay one half on its flat side. Keeping the root end intact, slice vertically from the root end following the onion's striated lines, then slice horizontally. To mince, slice more finely in each direction.

To dice a root vegetable such as a carrot, cut across into 2-inch lengths or longer. Cut each section in half length-wise. Place flat side down and slice vertically into 3 or 4 sections, then cut horizontally into small cubes.

Roll or Triangle Cut - This is used primarily for root veg-etables such as carrot, daikon, or parsnip. Slice the veg-etable in a diagonal. Roll it a quarter turn away from you and slice down. Continue with a diagonal cut and so on.

The Spice and Herb Rack

Herbs and spices have been a part of traditional medicine for centuries. Their provocative aroma stimulates the appetite while their healing qualities aid in digestion.

Spices consist of the seeds, fruit, pods, bark, and buds of plants. Hot spices such as ginger, cayenne, chili, and mustard are used traditionally as a stimulant and as a cleansing aid for toxins.

Spices such as allspice, cloves, cinnamon, coriander, ginger, nutmeg and mace add a warming, expansive quality to foods. They compliment sweet foods such as winter squashes, yams, sweet potatoes, desserts and fruit dishes.

Herbs enhance the simplest dish by adding flavor and aroma. Fresh herbs can easily be grown in a garden or even a windowsill.

The following spices and herbs are used in my recipes:

SPICES
Allspice - These small, dried berries come from a South American tree and have a taste similar to cloves, nutmeg and cinnamon. For best flavor, freshly grind the whole berries. Allspice is known to relieve digestive problems, including flatulence.

Caraway - These seeds have a sweet, aniseed flavor that are traditionally used in cabbage as they counteract its gas-forming tendencies. Caraway can also be used for menstrual cramps.

Cayenne - This comes from a pod and seeds of a variety of chili pepper and is sometimes referred to as red pepper. This hot, reddish-brown powder does not add much flavor to foods but instead contributes color and heat to curries, soups, and stews. Cayenne is a stimulant, known for its antiseptic and digestive properties to improve blood circulation. Too much, however, may irritate the stomach.

Chili - Dried chili is hotter than fresh and comes in powder and flake forms. Choose chili powder without added ingredients such as onion or garlic. In traditional medicine, it is used as a stimulant and expectorant.

Cinnamon - This is available in sticks and ground. The stick form compliments sweet dishes and fruits, as well as pilafs, curries, and couscous. It contains certain properties that are antibacterial.

Cloves - These are actually the unopened buds of ever-green trees from Southeast Asia. It is usually combined with cinnamon to flavor desserts and hot mulled apple cider. Its oil has anesthetic qualities and is commonly used to soothe toothaches and other pains.

Coriander - This is an essential ingredient in Indian curries. As a powder, it loses its flavor and aroma quickly so it is best to use freshly bought. The seeds can be dry roasted to bring out its flavor, and then ground in a mortar and pestle or coffee mill. It has traditionally been used as a digestive aid, for diarrhea, and nausea.

Cumin - Along with coriander, this is part of Indian curries. The bitterness of the seeds is tamed by dry roasting them and the result is more flavorful than the powder. Because of its digestive properties, it works well with beans.

Ginger - For centuries, the fresh root has been used medicinally for its ability to help break down the uric acid in high protein foods such as animal foods and beans. When prepared as a tea, ginger's warming qualities relieve motion sickness, vomiting, morning sickness, spasms, colds and menstrual cramps. Both its root and powder add a sweet and spicy flavor to soups, vegetable dishes, sauces, fruits and baked goods.

Mustard - The 3 different types of seed are white, brown and black, which is the strongest. Crush the seeds to release their flavor and aroma or sauté them in oil before adding them to dishes. Add the sautéed seeds toward the end of the cooking process as they lose their flavor and intensity with time and cooking. This hot spice is used traditionally for colds and flu.

Nutmeg and Mace - Mace is the membrane that surrounds the nutmeg seed. Both have similar sweet flavors that are typically used to flavor pastries, oatmeal and vegetables. For a superior taste, freshly grind the whole seed. The powder form loses its flavor with time. It improves appetite and digestion when taken in small amounts and acts as a hallucinogenic when overused.

Paprika - This is a mild variety of cayenne. It adds flavor and heat to foods and has a digestive stimulant and antiseptic properties. In small amounts it can improve blood circulation.

Turmeric - This adds not only a yellow color to foods; it contributes an earthy, bitter flavor to curries and stews. It has important antioxidant and anti-inflammatory qualities and helps to protect the liver from toxins.

Vanilla - The vanilla bean has a sweet, almost intoxicating scent. It can be re-used by rinsing and pat drying, then storing in an airtight container. The extract is prepared only with alcohol unlike the artificial vanilla flavoring, which has many additives and not nearly the same wonderful taste.

Buying and Storing - Purchase in small amounts to insure freshness. Its aroma indicates its freshness. Store in airtight jars in a cool place away from direct light and heat.

HERBS

Basil is widely used in Italian and Thai dishes and is the basic ingredient in pesto sauce. Its delicate taste is best achieved by using the whole leaf or by tearing rather than cutting with a knife. It is known to aid in digestion and to calm upset stomachs and nausea.

Bay Leaves are used to flavor lentils and tomato based sauces. Their strong spicy flavor is enhanced when dried. They are known to aid in digestion.

Chives belong to the onion family although they have a much milder taste. These are added to grain and vegetable dishes. As with onions, chives act as a digestive with antiseptic properties.

Cilantro, also known as coriander, looks similar to parsley but the taste is very different; it is more spicy and flavorful. It is used in curries and as an alternative to parsley in stir-fries. Freshly minced adds color and flavor to grain and vegetable salads. Its root has a stronger flavor than the leaves and is used in soup stock and curry paste. Cilantro is suggested as a digestive aid and to treat nausea.

Dill has a mild flavor and long, feathered leaves similar to anise. It is popularly used in potato salad, grain salads and with cucumbers. Its delicate taste is lost when cooked, so it must be added at the end of the cooking process.

Garlic Chives are the tops of the garlic plant and are widely used in China. Their taste is milder than garlic and can be used like chives or added to stir-fry at the end of the cooking process.

Mint has many varieties. The most familiar are spearmint, and peppermint. It is used in many dishes such as tea, desserts, stuffing, fruit and vegetable salads, grain dishes and yogurt. It is a cure for digestive problems and is also known to stimulate and cleanse the body.

Parsley has 2 types of leaves - flat and curly. They taste the same, but the flat leaf is used mostly in cooked dishes. It is one of the highest sources of vitamin C and is also high in iron and calcium.

Storing - Place the stems either in a glass jar half filled with water or dampen a paper towel and wrap the roots in it, then place in a plastic bag in the fridge. You can also freeze fresh herbs by chopping them, then packing them in plastic containers.

Hint - Add herbs last when cooking to avoid bitter flavor.

COCONUT CUISINE 26

RECIPES

Stevia GingerLemonade

Because this is an essential liquid ingredient in many of my recipes, I have included various methods for its preparation in a chapter of its own.

This tea can be brewed using either stevia flow-thru teabags or by placing loose cut stevia leaves in a re-use-able cotton teabag or a tea ball. Use spring water.

cool water brew: To one quart of room temperature water, add 2 stevia teabags or 3 tsp. cut leaf. Add 1/3 cup freshly squeezed lemon juice and 1 1/2 to 2 TB fresh ginger juice. Allow to steep for 3 to 4 hours. Remove teabags and refrigerate. After it has chilled for a few hours, it is ready to drink; the sweetness has mellowed and blended with the other ingredients. If the taste is too sweet, add more lemon juice.

hot water brew: Teabags added to hot water result in a stronger taste and require time to smooth it out. Add 4 stevia teabags or 2 TB cut leaf to half gallon of water. Heat just until very hot to the touch. Let cool, then remove the tea bags. Add at least 1/2 cup lemon juice and 1 1/2 to 2 TB ginger juice. Allow flavors to mellow in the fridge until cold. Add more lemon juice if too sweet.

sun brew: Same proportions as above. Add all ingredients together and put in the sun to brew. Remove tea bags after a few hours.

mint brew: Include 1/2 to 1 cup fresh mint leaves to same proportions as above. This brew is exceptional served either hot or cold.

Instant non-brew method

To 8 oz. of plain or effervescent spring water, add 6 to 10 drops stevia clear liquid or liquid concentrate, or a dusting of extract and desired amount of lemon and ginger juice.

Stevia Marinade

To 8 oz. of spring water, add 8 to 10 drops stevia clear liquid, 1/4 cup lemon juice and 1 tsp. ginger juice.

Ginger juice

The Japanese porcelain round ginger grater is a superior tool for making ginger juice and is a real pleasure to use. Otherwise, there are several other ginger graters on the market, or use a garlic press or a fine grater. Grate desired amount of washed, unpeeled fresh ginger root, gather the gratings in your fist and squeeze out the juice. Discard pulp.

Hints

Lime juice or a combination of lemon/lime juice can be substituted for lemon juice.

Place used teabags over your eyes for a soothing effect.

Home-Made Liquid Concentrate

1.   One cup of warm spring water in a glass jar or other non-reactive container.

2.   Add 1/4 cup of stevia leaf powder or grind the cut leaves in a blender or coffee mill.

3.   Let set 24 to 48 hours.

4.   Strain through cheesecloth to remove all leaves and sediment.

5.   Repeat steps 2, 3 and 4 to make a sweeter liquid.

6.   Keep refrigerated.

7.   Put into a 1-ounce dropper bottle to carry with you.

COCONUT CUISINE 30

BREAKFAST

BREAKFAST

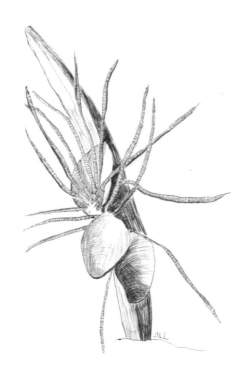

Scrambled Tofu

serves 4

Tofu is a low-fat, digestible protein, providing B-vitamins, calcium, iron and potassium. Including vegetables and healing spices such as garlic and ginger promotes a healthy start to your day.

8 oz.	soft tofu
	coconut oil for sautéing
	chopped garlic or ginger
8 oz.	ground cumin
1 large	carrot, diced
2 ears	corn, remove kernels
1 cup	red cabbage, finely chopped
2 drops	stevia clear liquid added to 1/4 cup water
to taste	tamari, shoyu, or sea salt
3	green onions, sliced diagonally

1 Crumble the tofu in a bowl.
2 Heat the oil, add the garlic or ginger and cumin and sauté for 1 minute. Add stevia water and vegetables and sauté for 2 minutes. Add the tofu and shoyu, tamari or salt, cover and allow to steam for 5 minutes. Remove cover and stir in green onions.
3 Can be served with a grain or with toast.

Nutrition Facts – 1 Serving	
Calories 142.98	**% Daily Value**
Total Fat 5.74g	8%
Saturated Fat 0.81g	4%
Cholesterol 0.00mg	0%
Sodium 139.20mg	5%
Potassium 432.42mg	12%
Carbohydrates 20.41g	6%
Dietary Fiber 3.32g	13%
Protein 5.70g	11%
Vitamin A 5940.09IU	118%
Vitamin C 15.78mg	26%

Cooking Tips

Eat only moderate amounts of tofu. Over indulgence can cause weak kidneys.

Apricot Coconut Spread

yields 1 cup

1 cup	dried apricots
1/2 cup	hot spring water
1 cup	coconut milk
1 or more TB	coconut spread

1   Place apricots in hot water. Let stand for 30 minutes until they soften. Drain and reserve water for another use.

2   Purée apricots and coconut milk in a blender or food processor. Remove mixture to a bowl and blend in the coconut spread.

Nutrition Facts – 1 Serving	
Calories 239.59 **% Daily Value**	
Total Fat 16.90g	26%
Saturated Fat 14.87g	74%
Cholesterol 0.00mg	0%
Sodium 14.45mg	0%
Potassium 625.18mg	17%
Carbohydrates 24.16g	8%
Dietary Fiber 4.24g	16%
Protein 2.75g	5%
Vitamin A 2353.001UI	47%

Amaranth and Quinoa

serves 4

Amaranth and quinoa are the highest in protein of any grain. Because of amaranth's glutinous texture, this porridge is ever so warming and comforting.

2/3 cup	amaranth
2/3 cup	quinoa
2 1/2 cups	spring water
pinch	sea salt
	stevia clear liquid or extract
	coconut milk or coconut cream

1 Wash the quinoa in a metal strainer to eliminate its bitter surface. Because the amaranth grains are so small they should be washed in a dense metal strainer. (If you don't have one, then wash both together.)
2 Place the water, grains and salt in a saucepan. Bring to a boil, lower heat and simmer until the water is absorbed, about 15 to 20 minutes.
3 Sweeten to taste, if desired, and drizzle coconut milk or cream on top.

Nutrition Facts – 1 Serving	
Calories 110.59 % DailyValue	
Total Fat 1.68g	2%
Saturated Fat 0.18g	0%
Cholesterol 0.00mg	0%
Sodium 12.15mg	0%
Potassium 350.69mg	10%
Carbohydrates 20.43g	6%
Dietary Fiber 1.67g	6%
Protein 4.18g	8%

Creamy Oatmeal
serves 4

1 cup	rolled oats
4 cups	spring water
1/4 tsp.	fresh ground nutmeg
pinch	sea salt
	coconut flakes
	coconut milk or cream

1 Place oats, water, nutmeg and salt in a saucepan. Bring to a boil, lower heat and simmer for 15 to 20 minutes or longer until thick and creamy, stirring occasionally. Add stevia to taste, if needed.
2 Sprinkle each serving with coconut flakes and drizzle coconut milk or cream on top.

Nutrition Facts – 1 Serving	
Calories 110.59 % DailyValue	
Total Fat 5.74g	8%
Saturated Fat 0.81g	4%
Cholesterol 0.00mg	0%
Sodium 139.20mg	5%
Potassium 432.42mg	12%
Carbohydrates 20.41g	6%
Dietary Fiber 3.32g	13%
Protein 5.70g	11%

Fig Spread
serves 5

Fresh figs can be substituted for dried ones.

8	dried figs, diced (about 1 cup)
1 1/4 cups	coconut milk
2 TB	coconut spread
4 tsp.	coconut flakes
1/4 to 1/2 tsp.	ground cloves

1 Soften figs by soaking them in warmed coconut milk. Let sit for 15 minutes.
2 Blend all ingredients in a food processor or blender. Add coconut flakes. If desired, add coarsely ground walnuts or almonds.

Nutrition Facts – 1 Serving	
Calories 224.12 **% Daily Value**	
Total Fat 15.76g	24%
Saturated Fat 13.72g	68%
Cholesterol 0.00mg	0%
Sodium 11.81mg	0%
Potassium 367.33mg	10%
Carbohydrates 22.98g	7%
Dietary Fiber 4.80g	19%
Protein 2.45g	4%

Date Spread
serves 4

6	Medjool dates, pitted then diced
3/4 cup	coconut milk
1/4 tsp. or to taste	allspice
3 TB	coconut spread

1 Blend dates, coconut milk and allspice.
2 Remove to a bowl and blend in the coconut spread.

Nutrition Facts – 1Serving	
Calories 154.84 **% Daily Value**	
Total Fat 13.00g	19%
Saturated Fat 11.50g	57%
Cholesterol 0.00mg	0%
Sodium 6.33mg	0%
Potassium 210.96mg	6%
Carbohydrates 11.09g	3%
Dietary Fiber 1.18g	4%
Protein 1.51g	3%

Coconut Banana Porridge
serves 4

3	green bananas
2 cups	spring water
1 cup	coconut milk
1/2 tsp.	cinnamon
1/2 tsp.	freshly grated nutmeg
2 TB	whole wheat flour or other whole meal flour
	any form of stevia sweetened to taste
	coconut cream

1   Peel the green bananas by slicing off both ends then splitting them lengthwise cutting through to the flesh and peeling off the skins.

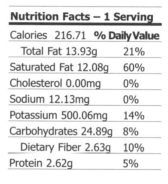

Nutrition Facts – 1 Serving

Calories 216.71	% Daily Value
Total Fat 13.93g	21%
Saturated Fat 12.08g	60%
Cholesterol 0.00mg	0%
Sodium 12.13mg	0%
Potassium 500.06mg	14%
Carbohydrates 24.89g	8%
Dietary Fiber 2.63g	10%
Protein 2.62g	5%

2   Purée bananas, water and coconut milk in a blender. Pour into a saucepan.

3   Blend flour with a little water to form a thin paste.

4   Bring the bananas to boil over a medium heat and simmer for 15 to 20 minutes until the mixture is cooked. Add the cinnamon, nutmeg and flour mixture. Stir frequently until the porridge thickens. Cook for 10 more minutes.

5   Serve in bowls, blend in desired amount of stevia and add a dollop of coconut cream on top.

JILL

COCONUT CUISINE 38

APPETIZERS

APPETIZERS

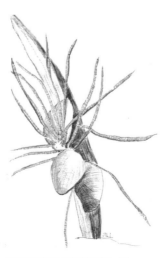

Baba Ganoosh
serves 4/yields 1 1/3 cups

1 large	eggplant
3 level tsp.	sesame tahini
1 level tsp.	coconut spread
1/2 tsp.	garlic, or more to taste, peeled and crushed with sea salt
3 TB	lemon juice or more to taste
2 drops	stevia clear liquid, or to taste
3 to 4 TB	cold spring water
1/2 tsp.	sea salt

Garnish

hot Hungarian paprika
chopped parsley or cilantro
diced ripe tomatoes (optional)

1   Pierce eggplant in several places with a toothpick. Wrap in tin foil and place in a 375 degree F. oven for 30 to 40 minutes, until it is soft.

2   Squeeze pulp to remove any bitter juices. Remove the pulp and mash to a purée.

3   In a food processor, combine the tahini and coconut spread with the garlic, lemon juice and stevia and blend until smooth. Thin with the water. With the machine running, add the eggplant and the salt.

4   Spread out in a shallow dish and add the garnishes.

Nutrition Facts – 1 Serving	
Calories 42.16	**% Daily Value**
Total Fat 2.85g	4%
Saturated Fat 0.70g	3%
Cholesterol 0.00mg	0%
Sodium 239.88mg	9%
Potassium 98.32mg	2%
Carbohydrates 4.01g	1%
Dietary Fiber 1.19g	4%
Protein 1.25g	2%

Avocado Spread
serves 1

Serve as a sandwich with lettuce, sprouts and tomato, or as a dip for raw vegetables.

1	Hass avocado
1 TB	coconut spread
1/4 cup	Vidalia onion, diced
few pinches	ground cumin
	sea salt to taste
1/4 cup	lemon juice or to taste
2 drops	stevia clear liquid

1 In a bowl, mash avocado pulp with a fork. Blend in the coconut spread, cumin and sea salt.
2 In a cup, combine lemon juice with stevia.
3 Combine all ingredients and blend well. Adjust seasonings to taste.

Nutrition Facts – 1 Serving	
Calories 185.46 **% Daily Value**	
Total Fat 17.62	27%
Saturated Fat 4.55g	22%
Cholesterol 0.00mg	0%
Sodium 293.28mg	12%
Potassium 604.18mg	17%
Carbohydrates 8.20g	2%
Dietary Fiber 4.76g	19%
Protein 2.33g	4%

Coconut Raita
serves 2

This East Indian dish is traditionally prepared with a homemade yogurt that has the same consistency as this coconut milk version.

1 small	cucumber, peeled
6 oz.	coconut milk
3 TB	lemon juice
2 or more drops	stevia clear liquid
1/4 tsp.	cumin

1 Slice the cucumber in half lengthwise and remove the seeds. Either grate the cucumber or thinly slice it.
2 Combine other ingredients in a bowl and add the cucumber slices. Refrigerate.

Nutrition Facts – 1 Serving	
Calories 200.72 **% Daily Value**	
Total Fat 19.50g	30%
Saturated Fat 17.09g	85%
Cholesterol 0.00mg	0%
Sodium 15.40mg	0%
Potassium 451.25mg	12%
Carbohydrates 7.84g	2%
Dietary Fiber 1.17g	4%
Protein 2.81g	5%

Basil Coconut Spread
serves 4

Spread on crudités or on warm rye bread, sprinkled with coconut flakes.

1/2 cup	fresh basil leaves
1 TB.	coconut oil
1/2 tsp.	umeboshi paste or 1 to 2 TB lemon juice
1 TB	golden flax seeds, ground in a coffee mill or blender
2 to 4 drops	stevia clear liquid
	coconut flakes for garnish

1 Blend all ingredients except coconut flakes in a food processor. Garnish with coconut flakes.

Nutrition Facts – 1 Serving	
Calories 72.80 **% Daily Value**	
Total Fat 6.08g	9%
Saturated Fat 4.52g	22%
Cholesterol 0.00mg	0%
Sodium 3.85mg	0%
Potassium 84.81mg	2%
Carbohydrates 4.40g	1%
Dietary Fiber 1.04g	4%
Protein 1.10g	2%

Carrot Aspic
serves 6

This can also be served as a refreshing side dish for any main course.

3 cups	carrots, cleaned and grated
1 1/2 cups	spring water
1 1/2 cup	coconut milk
1 TB	ginger juice
1/4 tsp.	sea salt
3 pinches	ground cloves
1/4 tsp.	ground cumin
3 to 5 drops	stevia clear liquid or light dusting of stevia extract
3 full TB	agar-agar flakes
3 TB	lemon juice

1   Cook the carrots in spring water until tender.

2   Place spring water and cooked carrots in a blender. Add all ingredients except agar and lemon juice and purée.

3   Transfer to a saucepan, add the agar and bring to a boil. Simmer for 10 minutes until agar is completely dissolved. Remove from heat and add the lemon juice.

4   Rinse out a mold or a square glass or ceramic dish and pour in the mixture. Allow to cool. Place in the refrigerator until it firms.

Nutrition Facts – 1 Serving	
Calories 158.75 **% Daily Value**	
Total Fat 12.22g	18%
Saturated Fat 10.71g	53%
Cholesterol 0.00mg	0%
Sodium 115.88mg	4%
Potassium 408.69mg	11%
Carbohydrates 13.42g	4%
Dietary Fiber 2.41g	9%
Protein 2.21g	11%
Vitamin A 18005.20IU	360%

Faux Foie Gras
serves 6/yields 3 cups

These legumes have a sweet flavor and are easily digestible. They act as a mild laxative and diuretic and benefit the liver, stomach and spleen. They are also known to aid in hiccups.

1 cup	dried split peas, soaked overnight
3 cups	spring water
1 piece	kombu sea vegetable, quickly rinsed
1/4 tsp.	sea salt
6 oz.	button mushrooms, sliced
1 medium	onion, diced
1 TB	coconut oil
1/4 tsp	cumin powder
1/8 tsp.	stevia cut leaves or a dusting of extract
1 cup	fresh squeezed lemon juice, or to taste

1   Eliminate the soaking water and rinse the peas. Place them in a large pot, add water and kombu, cover and bring to a boil. Scoop off any foam that rises to the top. Turn heat to low, add cumin and stevia and cook until the peas are 80% cooked. Add the salt and continue cooking until peas are soft. Total cooking time about 40 minutes.
2   Sauté onions in oil until translucent. Add mushrooms and a pinch of salt and continuing sautéing until tender.
3   Purée peas, onions, mushrooms and lemon juice in a blender.

Cooking Tips

Cumin helps prevent gas while the lemon juice makes the legumes more digestible. Since salt prevents legumes from cooking, it is added at the end of the cooking process. By adding a proportion of 5 or 6 times spring water to the split peas, this pâté becomes a soup.

Nutrition Facts – 1 Serving	
Calories 147.73 **% Daily Value**	
Total Fat 2.79g	4%
Saturated Fat 2.79g	1%
Cholesterol 0.00mg	0%
Sodium 92.59mg	3%
Potassium 462.03mg	13%
Carbohydrates 22.94g	7%
Dietary Fiber 9.11g	36%
Protein 9.16g	18%
Folate 100.18µg	25%

Mango Salsa
serves 4/yields 1 cup

Spread on celery, fennel or bell pepper wedges. Or, peel a cucumber, scoop out the seeds and fill.

Salsa

1	slightly under-ripe mango; dice the pulp
4 TB	sweet onion, diced
1/4 cup	red bell pepper, diced
1 tsp.	coconut flakes
1 TB	cilantro, minced
	juice of 1 or more limes

Dressing

1 tsp.	ginger juice
1 to 2 drops	stevia clear liquid
pinch each	sea salt
	cayenne pepper
	ground cumin

Nutrition Facts – 1 Serving	
Calories 51.08 **% Daily Value**	
Total Fat 0.82g	1%
Saturated Fat 0.55g	2%
Cholesterol 0.00mg	0%
Sodium 73.55mg	3%
Potassium 139.61mg	3%
Carbohydrates 12.21g	4%
Dietary Fiber 1.91g	7%
Protein 0.67g	1%
Vitamin A 2431.50IU	48%
Vitamin C 31.27mg	52%

1   Combine all dressing ingredients in a cup and adjust taste if necessary.
2   Mix salsa ingredients and dressing together in a glass or ceramic bowl and allow to marinate for at least 30 minutes.

Cooking Tips
Feel free to add any other spices or seasonings.

Hijiki Spread
yields about a cup

Serve small mounds on slices of garlic-roasted baguettes or fill celery, fennel sticks, sautéed button mushrooms, or hollowed out cucumbers.

1 oz.	hijiki sea vegetable
1 small	garlic clove, peeled
1/2 cup	black olives, pitted
3 TB	capers
1 to 2 TB	coconut oil
2 TB	lemon juice
	fresh mint or thyme
	leaves for garnish

Nutrition Facts – 1 Serving	
Calories 54.95 **% Daily Value**	
Total Fat 5.75g	8%
Saturated Fat 4.09g	20%
Cholesterol 0.00mg	0%
Sodium 239.54mg	9%
Potassium 9.75mg	0%
Carbohydrates 1.49g	0%
Dietary Fiber 0.52g	2%
Protein 0.25g	0%

1   Place hijiki strands in a large bowl and pour enough boiling spring water on top to cover by 2 inches. Leave for 15 minutes, until softened. Drain and reserve water for soup
2   In a food processor, add garlic, then hijiki, olives, capers and oil. Process to create a course paste, scraping down the sides of the bowl as needed.
3   Add enough lemon juice and salt, if needed, to give it an assertive flavor.
4   Transfer to a bowl and garnish with mint or thyme.

Leek Pâté

serves 4 to 6/yields 1 1/3 cups

3 large or	leeks, tender green and white parts, washed,
6 medium	trimmed, and sliced 1/8-inch thick
1/4 tsp.	sea salt or to taste
3 cloves	garlic, unpeeled
1/2 cup	walnuts, chopped
pinch	hot Hungarian paprika
1/2 tsp.	ground coriander seeds
1/3 cup	mixed chopped herbs: basil, celery tops, and mint
2 tsp.	lemon juice
	coconut cream

1   Steam leeks until almost tender. Add the garlic and cook 2 minutes longer. Remove garlic, peel, set aside.

2   Drain the leeks and let cool. Squeeze them over a bowl to extract as much liquid as possible; reserve 2 TB of the liquid. Coarsely chop the leeks and transfer to a bowl.

3   In a mortar or coffee grinder, grind walnuts with sea salt, garlic, ground coriander seeds and cayenne. Grind until the mixture is pasty. Remove to a bowl and blend in the 2 TB leek spring water.

4   Add the walnut mixture to the leeks and, using your fingers, mix in the coriander seeds, paprika, and herbs.

5   Moisten the mixture with the lemon juice. Adjust seasonings to taste, if necessary.

6   Pack firmly into a lightly oiled 1 1/2-cup bowl and cover tightly and refrigerate at least a few hours or overnight.

7   To serve, bring to room temperature and invert onto a serving plate. Drizzle with coconut cream.

Nutrition Facts – 1 Serving	
Calories 107.68 **% Daily Value**	
Total Fat 7.64g	11%
Saturated Fat 1.41g	7%
Cholesterol 0.00mg	0%
Sodium 166.78mg	6%
Potassium 206.73mg	5%
Carbohydrates 9.11g	3%
Dietary Fiber 2.18g	8%
Protein 2.77g	5%

Stuffed Cucumber
serves 2

This simple and refreshing dish also combines well with other herbs such as rosemary, dill, savory, tarragon, basil or mint. A hint of sweetness, compliments the flavor of herbs and lemon rind.

1	cucumber - choose a cucumber that is small and wide, 4" to 5" long.
2	olives, finely chopped
1	garlic clove, minced
few sprigs	fresh thyme, minced
few sprigs	cilantro or parsley, minced

Dressing: combine in a cup

1 TB	coconut oil
1 TB	lemon juice or more
few	fine gratings of lemon peel
2 pinches	sea salt
1 drop	stevia clear liquid
or half a pinch	ground leaf stevia

1   Cut a 1/3-inch slice off one end of the cucumber, dip in sea salt and rub both ends together in a circular motion. This will bring any bitter foam to the surface. Wash off and repeat with the other side.

2   Peel the cucumber and cut in half lengthwise. Scoop out the seeds and pulp with a spoon.

3   Finely chop the cucumber skin, the seeds and pulp. Place in a bowl with the olives, garlic and herbs. Blend in the dressing.

Nutrition Facts – 1 Serving	
Calories 102.118 **% Daily Value**	
Total Fat 7.71g	11%
Saturated Fat 1.10g	5%
Cholesterol 0.00mg	0%
Sodium 332.79mg	13%
Potassium 332.79mg	9%
Carbohydrates 8.85g	2%
Dietary Fiber 3.28g	13%
Protein 1.84g	3%
Vitamin C 32.85mg	54%

4   Fill the hollowed cucumber halves with the mixture and allow flavors to meld for 15 minutes in the fridge.

Cooking Tips

If there is any filling left over, use it to fill a celery stick, a wedge of sweet bell pepper, or as a filling for sautéed button mushrooms.

Spinach Aspic
serves 4

Can also be served as an accompaniment to any main-course.

4 cups	spring water
1 lb.	spinach, cleaned well, stems trimmed
1 medium	carrot, hand grated on large size grate
4 TB	coconut milk
few pinches	sea salt
few pinches	ground nutmeg
4 TB	agar-agar
8 to 10 drops	stevia liquid
	coconut oil

1   Boil the water, add the spinach and carrots and cook for 3 minutes. Drain the vegetables well in a strainer by pressing out the liquid. Return the cooking water to the pot.

2   Add the agar and stevia to the cooking water. Bring to a slow boil and let simmer for 5 minutes, until the agar dissolves, stirring occasionally.

3   In a bowl, crush the spinach with the back of a fork and finely chop any long stems. Add the carrots, nutmeg and salt and blend well, then blend in the coconut milk.

4   Oil either a 1-quart, non-metallic mold or shallow square pan. Evenly distribute the spinach and carrot mixture on the bottom of the pan. Pour the agar water over the vegetables.

5   Let it cool completely, or place in the refrigerator when it begins to cool off.

6   Unmold with the tip of a knife. Serve with slices of radishes or onions.

Nutrition Facts – 1 Serving	
Calories 66.65 **% Daily Value**	
Total Fat 3.65g	5%
Saturated Fat 0.81g	14%
Cholesterol 0.00mg	0%
Sodium 108.38mg	4%
Potassium 757.42mg	21%
Carbohydrates 7.26g	2%
Dietary Fiber 3.89g	15%
Protein 3.84g	7%
Vitamin A 15350.29IU	307%
Vitamin C 34.57mg	57%
Folate 227.38µg	56%

SOUPS
&
STEWS

SOUPS & STEWS

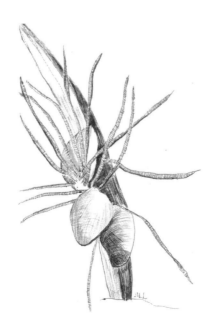

Spicy Pumpkin Soup
serves 4

Pumpkin (or winter squash) has a naturally sweet flavor that satisfies the craving for artificial sweeteners without affecting blood sugar levels. Its warming qualities nourish the spleen-pancreas and stomach. Besides being low in calories, it provides an excellent source of magnesium, potassium, calcium and vitamins A and C. If Hokkaido pumpkin is not available, use buttercup or kabocha squash.

	spring water
1	Hokkaido pumpkin, washed, unpeeled, seeded and cubed
1	onion, diced
3 inch piece	kombu or alaria sea vegetable, rinsed and soaked in water to cover for 15 minutes
2 inch piece	ginger root, washed
1/4 tsp. each	turmeric, curry, cumin
1/4 tsp.	ground leaf stevia or 3 to 5 drops clear liquid
1/4 tsp.	sea salt
	coconut milk
	tamari roasted pumpkin seeds for garnish

1   In a pot, combine all ingredients except the sea salt and coconut milk. Add the seaweed soaking water plus enough spring water to cover 1 to 2 inches above vegetables. Cook until squash is soft, about 30 minutes. The more water you add, the thinner the consistency.
2   Just before the pumpkin is nearly cooked, add sea salt.
3   Remove ginger root and purée in batches in a blender.
4   Drizzle coconut milk on top of each serving and garnish with roasted pumpkin seeds.

Cooking Tips

The same rule applies to squash as to all legumes: do not add salt until 80 % cooked. Salt stops the cooking process.

When choosing squash, look for one that feels heavy for its size. The pulp should have a dark, orange color indicating a sweet, rich flavor. A weak color produces a weak taste.

The peel, which contains many vitamins and minerals, can be eaten if it is organic.

Nutrition Facts – 1 Serving	
Calories 93.04	% Daily Value
Total Fat 3.55g	5%
Saturated Fat 0.70g	3%
Cholesterol 0.00mg	0%
Sodium 204.45mg	8%
Potassium 465.58mg	13%
Carbohydrates 13.17g	4%
Dietary Fiber 1.87g	7%
Protein 4.49g	8%
Vitamin A 1431.98IU	28%

Buttercup Stew
serves 6

Acorn squash or butternut squash can be substituted.

2 1/2 lbs.	buttercup squash
3 cups	coconut milk
1/2 tsp.	stevia clear liquid or a pinch of extract
pinch	sea salt
	roasted pumpkin seeds and mint sprigs, to decorate

1   Wash the squash skin. If organic, don't peel. Otherwise, peel off most of it. Scoop out the seeds.

2   Cut into about 2-inch pieces long and 1/4 inch thick.

3   In a saucepan, bring the coconut milk, stevia and salt to a boil. Add the pumpkin and simmer for 10 to 15 minutes, until the pumpkin is tender.

4   Serve warm. Garnish each serving with a mint sprig and a few toasted pumpkin seeds.

Nutrition Facts – 1 Serving	
Calories 313.23	% Daily Value
Total Fat 30.65g	47%
Saturated Fat 25.77g	128%
Cholesterol 0.00mg	0%
Sodium 19.33mg	0%
Potassium 518.02mg	14%
Carbohydrates 10.42g	3%
Dietary Fiber 3.07g	12%
Protein 4.79g	9%

Red Lentil and Coconut Soup
serves 4

This hearty soup is a meal in itself. Serve with crusty bread and a leafy green vegetable. Lentils are high in minerals, including iron and calcium, as well as folic acid, which is recommended for pregnant women.

2 TB	coconut oil
2	red onions, diced
1	chili pepper, seeded and minced
2 cloves	garlic, diced
1-inch piece	fresh lemongrass, outer leaves removed and inside finely sliced
1 tsp.	ground coriander
1 scant cup	red lentils
1 2/3 cup	coconut milk
1 tsp.	paprika
	juice of 1 lime
3	scallions, diced
1 scant cup	cilantro, finely chopped
	sea salt to taste

1   Heat oil in large, deep skillet and add the onions, chili, garlic and lemongrass. Sauté for 5 minutes or until the onions are soft, stirring occasionally.

2   Add lentils and spices, but not the salt. Pour in coconut milk and 3 3/4 cup spring water, and stir. Bring to a boil, stir, then reduce the heat and simmer for 30 minutes or until the lentils are soft.

3   Add the lime juice, scallions, cilantro and sea salt. Reserve some cilantro and scallions for garnish on individual servings.

Nutrition Facts – 1 Serving	
Calories 520.59 **% Daily Value**	
Total Fat 32.59g	50%
Saturated Fat 25.99g	129%
Cholesterol 12.60mg	4%
Sodium 12.60mg	10%
Potassium 675.96mg	19%
Carbohydrates 44.80g	14%
Dietary Fiber 6.58g	26%
Protein 18.43g	36%
Vitamin A 1271.51IU	25%
Iron 8.15 mg	45%
Folate 148.32µg	37%
Phosphorus 282.17mg	28%

Mung Bean Soup
serves 4

Mung beans are part of the kidney bean family. They are highly alkalizing and benefit the liver and gall bladder. Its cooling nature lends itself to warm summer days.

1 cup	dried mung beans, washed and soaked minimum 4 hours
1 strip	kombu sea vegetable, lightly washed and soaked 15 minutes
4 cups	spring water
1	carrot, diced
1	onion, diced
1/4 tsp.each	cumin and turmeric
1/4 tsp.	ground leaf stevia
1/4 tsp.	sea salt
	lemon juice
	coconut oil (optional)
	cilantro or parsley, minced

1   Drain and discard soaking water from beans and rinse. In a pot, combine water, beans, kombu and its soaking water. Cover and bring to a boil. Scoop off any foam that rises to the top.
2   Add carrots, onions, cumin, and turmeric. Simmer 1 hour or longer until creamy. Add sea salt and ground leaf stevia and cook 5 minutes longer.
3   Add fresh lemon juice and a splash of coconut oil to each serving and garnish with cilantro.

Nutrition Facts – 1 Serving	
Calories 202.30 **% Daily Value**	
Total Fat 2.06g	3%
Saturated Fat 0.23g	1%
Cholesterol 0.00mg	0%
Sodium 157.67mg	6%
Potassium 602.96mg	17%
Carbohydrates 34.18g	11%
Dietary Fiber 10.40g	41%
Protein 13.48g	26%
Vitamin A 5702.13IU	114%
Iron 4.21mg	25%
Folate 121.98µg	30%
Magnesium 148.35mg	37%

Cooking Tips
Dried split peas can be substituted for mung beans. Kombu not only adds essential minerals to the soup, it also breaks down the fibers and makes the beans more digestible.

Lentil Yam Stew
serves 4 to 6

This is a hearty and nourishing meal. Red lentils can be substituted for brown or green lentils. Their taste is similar, but with a creamier texture.

3 inch strip	kombu sea vegetable
3 to 5 cups	spring water
1 cup	brown or green lentils
1	yam, washed and cubed
1	onion, cubed
1/2 tsp. each	turmeric, cumin powder
1 inch piece	ginger root
1/4 tsp.	sea salt, or to taste
1/4 tsp.	stevia ground leaf

1   Wash salt off the kombu and place in a pot with enough spring water to cover for about 15 minutes, until it softens. Reserve the soaking water as part of the cooking water.

2   Wash lentils and place them in the pot with the water. Bring to a boil. With a spoon, remove any foam that rises to the top. Add all ingredients, except the salt, bring to a boil, then turn heat to low, cover and simmer.

3   The lentils will take about 30 to 40 minutes until they are soft. When they are about 80 % done, add the sea salt and continue cooking.

4   Discard the ginger; remove the kombu and slice into small bite-size pieces and return to the pot.

Nutrition Facts – 1 Serving

	% Daily Value
Calories 146.12	
Total Fat 0.78g	1%
Saturated Fat 0.15g	0%
Cholesterol 0.00mg	0%
Sodium 98.32mg	4%
Potassium 408.91mg	11%
Carbohydrates 27.23g	9%
Dietary Fiber 4.72g	18%
Protein 8.57g	17%

Cooking Tips
Since salt stops legumes from cooking, always add it near the end of the cooking process.

Cool Cucumber Mint Soup

serves 3

1 1/2 cups	cucumbers, peeled and chopped (2 medium cukes)
8 oz.	coconut milk
1 cup	loosely packed fresh mint leaves
1/4 cup	lemon juice
1 tsp.	stevia cut or powdered leaf
1/4 tsp.	sea salt

Nutrition Facts – 1 Serving	
Calories 176.64 **% Daily Value**	
Total Fat 17.25g	26%
Saturated Fat 15.18g	75%
Cholesterol 0.00mg	0%
Sodium 171.25mg	7%
Potassium 348.19mg	9%
Carbohydrates 6.94g	2%
Dietary Fiber 1.23g	4%
Protein 2.39g	4%
Vitamin C 14.73	25%

1   Add all ingredients in a food processor or blender. Pulse to begin blending, then blend until smooth. Chill. Add finely chopped cucumbers on each serving.

Polenta Soup

serves 8

1 cup	coarse grind cornmeal
2 large	onions, diced
2 medium	carrots, diced
4	scallions, diced
1/4 tsp.	fresh thyme
1 TB	coconut oil
10 cups	spring water
1/4 tsp.	sea salt

Nutrition Facts – 1 Serving	
Calories 92.69 **% Daily Value**	
Total Fat 2.35g	3%
Saturated Fat 1.56g	7%
Cholesterol 0.00mg	0%
Sodium 82.22mg	3%
Potassium 178.77mg	5%
Carbohydrates 16.99g	5%
Dietary Fiber 2.48g	9%
Protein 1.95g	3%
Vitamin A 5790.12IU	115%

1   Dry roast the polenta in a heavy skillet until it turns a golden brown, less than 10 minutes.

2   Sauté the vegetables in oil with a couple pinches of sea salt.

3   Boil the water and slowly add the polenta, stirring constantly to avoid lumps and until it becomes a creamy texture. Add the vegetables, thyme, and salt. Simmer for 40 to 50 minutes.

Millet Vegetable Stew

serves 4

Dry roasting the millet will result in a lighter texture.

1 cup	millet, washed
1 TB	coconut oil
1/2 cup	onions, sliced in half moons
1/2 cup	carrots, sliced in half moons
1/2 cup	Hokkaido pumpkin, buttercup or butternut squash (peeled), cut in cubes
3 cups	spring water
1/2 tsp.	sea salt

1   Dry roast the millet in a skillet on medium low heat until it becomes fragrant. Do not burn.

2   In a pressure cooker, heat the oil and sauté first the onion, then the carrot, and then the squash.

3   Cool the pan and add the millet, water and salt. Bring to pressure, turn down the heat to medium low, just so that it keeps the pressure throughout the cooking process. Cook for 20 minutes. Do not place under cold water. Let the pressure come down on its own.

4   If you're using a pot, bring to a boil and simmer for about 40 minutes.

Nutrition Facts – 1 Serving	
Calories 236.18	**% Daily Value**
Total Fat 5.60g	8%
Saturated Fat 3.32g	16%
Cholesterol 0.00mg	0%
Sodium 249.46mg	10%
Potassium 223.19mg	6%
Carbohydrates 4.60g	13%
Dietary Fiber 5.21g	20%
Protein 6.06g	12%
Vitamin A 5089.34IU	101%

Coconut Garlic Soup

serves 4 to 6

1 tsp.	coconut oil
6 cloves	garlic
	sea salt
1 medium	onion, diced
5 cups	vegetable stock or spring water
1 cup	coconut milk
pinch	ground cloves
pinch	cayenne pepper
2 to 4 drops	stevia clear liquid
	cilantro for garnish

1   Heat a heavy pot. Add coconut oil and heat. Add garlic and a pinch of sea salt and sauté for 1 minute.

2   Add onions, a pinch more sea salt and sauté until transparent.

3   Add stock or spring water, coconut milk, cloves, cayenne and stevia and continue to simmer until the soup becomes rich and creamy.

4   Transfer to a blender and purée. Garnish each bowl with chopped cilantro.

Nutrition Facts – 1 Serving

Calories 96.93	**% Daily Value**	
Total Fat 9.22g	14%	
Saturated Fat 8.11g	40%	
Cholesterol 0.00mg	0%	
Sodium 100.10mg	4%	
Potassium 128.89mg	3%	
Carbohydrates 3.97g	1%	
Dietary Fiber 0.44g	1%	
Protein 1.22g	2%	

SALADS

FORK KNIFE SPOON
MADE FROM COCONUT SHELL

SALADS ✻

Fruit and Coconut Salad with Creamy Mint Dressing

serves 2

Salad Ingredients

1 medium	orange, peeled and sectioned
1 medium	gala apple, sliced in thin sections, skin on if organic
1 small head	bib lettuce
1 tsp.	fresh lime juice or lemon juice
2 TB	coconut flakes
	chopped walnuts for garnish

Mint Cream Dressing

4 oz	soft tofu
2 TB	balsamic vinegar
1/3 cup or more	soymilk
1 TB	sweet white miso
1/2 cup	fresh mint leaves chopped
2 to 4 drops	stevia clear liquid

1   Place all dressing ingredients in a food processor or blender and blend until smooth. Adjust seasonings to taste. Start with 2 drops stevia and add more if necessary.

2   Place sliced oranges and apples in a bowl and add lemon or lime juice to prevent apples from turning brown.

3   On each plate, arrange half the orange and apple slices on top of the lettuce, sprinkle with coconut flakes, add the dressing and garnish with walnuts.

Nutrition Facts – 1 Serving	
Calories 272.49	**% Daily Value**
Total Fat 13.29g	20%
Saturated Fat 8.67g	43%
Cholesterol 0.00mg	0%
Sodium 567.91mg	23%
Potassium 773.84mg	22%
Carbohydrates 34.37g	11%
Dietary Fiber 8.89g	35%
Protein 9.50g	19%
Vitamin A 1276.08IU	25%
Vitamin C 59.97 mg	99%
Folate 103.61µg	25%

Cooking Tips

Basil, cilantro, parsley, dill or scallions can be substituted for mint.

Jicama, Apple & Celery
serves 4

Jicama (pronounced hicama) is sweet and juicy and tastes like an apple. Combined with celery, lemon juice, herbs and a touch of stevia, makes a refreshing summer salad.

1 small	jicama, peeled and cut into matchsticks
1 green	apple, cut into matchsticks
2 stalks	celery, thinly sliced on the diagonal
1/3 cup	cilantro or parsley, finely chopped

Dressing - combined in a cup

juice of 1 lemon

1 TB	balsamic, apple cider or umeboshi vinegar
4 drops	stevia clear liquid or 1/4 to 1/2 tsp. stevia cut or powdered leaf
1 tsp.	ginger juice (if desired)
	sea salt to taste

1 Combine dressing ingredients in a cup and adjust to taste.

2 Place salad ingredients in a bowl and add dressing. Allow flavors to blend.

Nutrition Facts – 1 Serving	
Calories 81.57 **% Daily Value**	
Total Fat 0.27g	0%
Saturated Fat 0.05g	0%
Cholesterol 0.00mg	0%
Sodium 100.08mg	4%
Potassium 424.23mg	12%
Carbohydrates 20.35g	6%
Dietary Fiber 5.25g	21%
Protein 1.26g	2%
Vitamin C 25.09mg	41%

Hijiki Salad
serves 4

This sea vegetable is high in calcium, iron, iodine, Vitamin B2 and niacin. It helps regulate blood sugar levels and has virtually no calories.

1 cup	hijiki strands
1 cup	carrots, cut into matchsticks
1 cup	daikon radish, cut into matchsticks
pinch	sea salt
1 cup	scallions, sliced diagonally
	coconut oil for sautéing
sea salt	
4 TB	roasted unhulled sesame seeds
	Stevia Marinade (pg. 29)

Dressing

2 to 4 TB	coconut oil
2 to 4 TB	Stevia Marinade

1   Combine Dressing ingredients in a cup.
2   Quickly rinse the hijiki. Place in a bowl and cover with spring water. Soak 10 minutes. Place in a saucepan with the soaking water and simmer 15 - 20 minutes. Drain, cool and cut into 2" pieces. Reserve soaking water for soup stock.
3   Heat skillet, add oil and heat. Add carrots, daikon and salt and sauté for one minute. Add about 1/3 cup of Marinade, 1/2 cup of the scallions and cook for a few minutes until liquid has evaporated. Transfer to a serving bowl.

4   Add the hijiki, remaining scallions, and sesame seeds. Add the dressing and toss. Allow to marinate for 30 minutes before serving.

Cooking Tips
Arame can be substituted for hijiki. Use all the hijiki soaking water except the bottom where dirt accumulates.

Nutrition Facts – 1 Serving	
Calories 207.63 **% Daily Value**	
Total Fat 17.27g	26%
Saturated Fat 7.40g	36%
Cholesterol 0.00mg	0%
Sodium 156.02mg	6%
Potassium 356.58mg	10%
Carbohydrates 12.46g	4%
Dietary Fiber 4.54g	18%
Protein 3.94g	7%
Vitamin A 9122.01IU	182%
Vitamin C 17.57mg	29%
Calcium 212.14mg	25%
Iron 3.40 mg	26%

❊ Edible Flower Salad
serves 4

Accenting this salad with brightly colored, edible flowers adds dimension and flavor.

1 bunch	watercress
1 bunch	arugula
1 large	avocado
3 stalks	green onions, thinly sliced diagonals
4 large	black olives, pitted and thinly sliced

Basic Salad Dressing (pg. 80)

nasturtium, marigold or other edible flowers

1   Wash, trim, and finely chop watercress and arugula. Dry thoroughly with a salad spinner or with paper towels.
2   Dice avocado and tomatoes.
3   Combine all ingredients, except the flowers, and blend in dressing. Accent with the flowers.

Nutrition Facts – 1 Serving	
Calories 147.75 **% Daily Value**	
Total Fat 11.75g	18%
Saturated Fat 3.25g	16%
Cholesterol 6.52mg	2%
Sodium 160.88mg	6%
Potassium 559.00mg	15%
Carbohydrates 8.47g	2%
Dietary Fiber 3.53g	14%
Protein 4.84g	9%
Vitamin C 26.07mg	43%

Marinated Cabbage Salad
serves 5

This can be served as either a side dish or an entrée.

3 cups	grated cabbage
1/2 cup	grated Vidalia onion
1/2 tsp.	sea salt
1 1/2 cups	grated green apple
1 1/2 cups	grated jicama
1 cup	finely chopped fresh basil leaves
1/4 cup	chopped walnuts (optional)

Dressing

1/2 cup	lemon juice
1/3 cup	coconut oil
1 tsp.	ground cumin
few pinches	cayenne pepper
3 to 5 drops	stevia clear liquid

1   Combine cabbage, onion and salt in a non-reactive bowl such as glass, ceramic or earthenware. Cover with the outer leaves of the cabbage and place a heavy object on top, such as a plate with a rock on it. The weight will release the water from the vegetables.
2   Leave for a few hours, occasionally draining off the excess water.
3   Add the basil and apple to the cabbage and onion and blend in the dressing. Garnish with chopped walnuts.

Nutrition Facts – 1 Serving

Calories 189.04	**% Daily Value**
Total Fat 15.01g	23%
Saturated Fat 12.63g	63%
Cholesterol 0.00mg	0%
Sodium 200.71mg	8%
Potassium 324.62mg	9%
Carbohydrates 15.51g	5%
Dietary Fiber 4.70g	18%
Protein 1.62g	3%
Vitamin C 40.17mg	66%

Berries, Avocado and Pecans in a Cinnamon and Lemon Dressing

serves 2

An intimate lunch for two...sensuous, colorful and spicy.

Salad Ingredients

1	Haas avocado, sliced into 6 sections
6 leaves	romaine lettuce
1/2 pint	strawberries, cleaned
1/2 pint	blueberries, cleaned
1 small	red onion, thinly sliced in half moons
1 or 2 TB	coconut flakes
1/4 cup	pecans, chopped

Dressing - combine in a cup

3 TB	coconut oil
1/4 tsp.	cinnamon
	juice of 1 lemon
2 pinches each	cayenne pepper, sea salt
2 to 4 drops	stevia clear liquid

1   Place 4 lettuce leaves on each serving plate. Sprinkle half of the berries, onions and coconut on top and drizzle on the dressing.

2   Arrange the avocado slices on top and add a pinch of sea salt and a few squeezes of lemon juice.

Nutrition Facts – 1 Serving	
Calories 616.24 **% Daily Value**	
Total Fat 51.87g	79%
Saturated Fat 25.05g	125%
Cholesterol 0.00mg	0%
Sodium 80.27mg	3%
Potassium 1194.00mg	34%
Carbohydrates 43.62g	14%
Dietary Fiber 15.25g	60%
Protein 6.44g	12%
Vitamin A 1485.58IU	29%
Vitamin C 156.54mg	260%

Parsley Potato Salad

serves 6

This taste even better the next day. Dill and mint will also compliment these potatoes.

2 lbs.	small red potatoes or Yukon gold variety
1	Vidalia, sweet or red onion, diced or cut into half moons
1/2 cup	parsley or cilantro, minced
	capers for garnish

Dressing - combine in a cup

1/4 to 1/3 cup	coconut oil
2 to 4 TB	apple cider or balsamic vinegar
2 drops	stevia clear liquid, or dusting of extract
	sea salt to taste

1   Slice potatoes into quarters (or larger size into eighths). Steam just until tender. Remove to bowl and allow to completely cool.

2   Combine the rest of the ingredients with the potatoes and mix in the dressing.

3   Allow flavors to blend. May need to readjust flavors before serving.

Nutrition Facts – 1 Serving	
Calories 242.48 **% Daily Value**	
Total Fat 9.08g	13%
Saturated Fat 1.23g	6%
Cholesterol 0.00mg	0%
Sodium 238.73mg	9%
Potassium 1105.77mg	31%
Carbohydrates 38.50g	12%
Dietary Fiber 3.04g	12%
Protein 4.10g	8%
Vitamin C 42.34mg	70%
Vitamin B6 0.51mg	25%

Cooking Tips

Wait until the potatoes have cooled before adding the dressing. Otherwise, they tend to soak up oil and become soggy.

Pomegranate Salad with Lemon Coconut Dressing

serves 4

Pomegranates have been reputed for millennia for their therapeutic properties to aid digestion, for stomach ailments and for sore eyes. Today they are acclaimed for their disease-fighting antioxidant potential. Preliminary studies suggest that pomegranate juice may contain almost three times the total antioxidant ability compared with the same quantity of green tea or red wine. It also provides a substantial amount of potassium, is high in fiber and contains vitamin C and niacin. Their sweet sour flavor is delicious sprinkled in puddings, cereals, vegetable dishes, baba ganoosh and hummus.

Dressing - combined in a cup

3 TB	coconut oil
1 1/2 TB	lemon juice
few pinches	sea salt
3 to 5 drops	stevia clear liquid
pinch	cayenne pepper

Salad

2 cups	mesclin salad greens
1 cup	fennel bulb, thinly sliced
	fresh orange segments
1/2 cup	pomegranate seeds

1   Arrange the salad ingredients on a serving plate and add the dressing.

Nutrition Facts – 1 Serving	
Calories 129.54	**% Daily Value**
Total Fat 10.38g	15%
Saturated Fat 8.85g	44%
Cholesterol 0.00mg	0%
Sodium 229.29mg	9%
Potassium 287.79mg	8%
Carbohydrates 10.29g	3%
Dietary Fiber 2.43g	9%
Protein 1.15g	2%
Vitamin C 28.09mg	46%

Purple Cabbage and Apple Salad

serves 3

I like to roll this salad in a sheet of toasted nori. It not only adds many essential minerals, it adds flavor and a colorful contrast.

	coconut oil for sautéing
1 TB	caraway seeds
1/2 head	purple cabbage, finely sliced or grated
	Stevia GingerLemonade or Stevia Marinade
1 small	green apple or other variety, grated
1 to 2 TB	coconut oil
1/4 cup	parsley or cilantro, minced
	sea salt to taste

1   Heat the oil in a skillet. Sauté the caraway seeds until they become fragrant. Add the cabbage, a pinch of sea salt and sauté on medium heat. Add just enough stevia liquid when needed to prevent burning. Sauté for about 10 minutes or until soft.

2   Transfer to a bowl and toss with apples, oil, parsley or cilantro and sea salt.

Nutrition Facts – 1 Serving

Calories 131.08	**% Daily Value**
Total Fat 9.66g	14%
Saturated Fat 1.28g	6%
Cholesterol 0.00mg	0%
Sodium 102.98mg	4%
Potassium 224.85mg	6%
Carbohydrates 11.93g	3%
Dietary Fiber 3.39g	13%
Protein 1.43g	2%
Vitamin C 38.26mg	63%

Cooking Tips

Caraway seeds not only add flavor to cabbage, they also help diminish cabbage's gas forming tendencies. For raw foodists, soak the caraway seeds overnight instead of sautéing them.

Cucumber Wakame Salad
serves 4

Wakame seaweed is very high in calcium, niacin and thiamine. The Japanese attribute their beautiful skin and lustrous, healthy hair to its properties.

1 cup	wakame
2	cucumbers - if using organic, do not peel.
1 tsp	shoyu or tamari
1/2 tsp	ginger juice, or ginger root peeled and grated
	juice of 1 lemon
1 to 3 drops	stevia clear liquid

1   Soak the wakame in enough spring water to cover for 5 minutes, or until soft. Trim off the middle rib and slice the wakame into 1/2 inch pieces. Use the rib for soups.

2   Cut a 1/3 inch slice off one end of the cucumber and rub both ends together in a circular motion. This will bring any bitter foam to the surface. Wash off and repeat with the other side. Cut in half lengthwise, then finely slice into half moons. Combine with the wakame in a bowl.

3   Combine other ingredients in a cup and pour over the wakame and cucumbers. Allow 30 minutes for the flavors to blend.

Nutrition Facts – 1 Serving	
Calories 27.14 **% Daily Value**	
Total Fat 0.30g	0%
Saturated Fat 0.08g	0%
Cholesterol 0.00mg	0%
Sodium 159.74mg	6%
Potassium 256.36mg	7%
Carbohydrates 6.04g	2%
Dietary Fiber 1.20g	4%
Protein 1.20g	2%

Cooking Tips
For a more delicate texture, peel the cucumbers and scoop out the seeds.

Cole Slaw
serves 4

1 tsp.	coconut oil
2 TB.	caraway seeds
1/2 head	green or purple cabbage - cored and finely sliced, or grated with the shredding disk of a food processor or the large holes of a hand grater.
2 large	carrots, grated
1 small	Vidalia or sweet onion, sliced in thin half moons
2 stalks	celery, thinly sliced diagonally
1/3 cup	sunflower seeds, roasted or pre-soaked
	dulse, raw or roasted
1 cup	Italian parsley, minced

Basic Salad Dressing (pg. 80)

1   Heat a skillet and add the oil. Sauté the caraway seeds until they pop and become fragrant.

2   Combine all ingredients in a serving bowl and blend with Basic Salad Dressing.

Cooking Tips

Caraway seeds not only add flavor to cabbage, they also help diminish cabbage's gas forming tendencies. For raw foodists, soak seeds overnight.

Nutrition Facts – 1 Serving	
Calories 127.24 **% Daily Value**	
Total Fat 8.39g	14%
Saturated Fat 0.91g	4%
Cholesterol 0.00mg	0%
Sodium 124.63mg	5%
Potassium 432.96mg	12%
Carbohydrates 11.56g	3%
Dietary Fiber 4.72g	18%
Protein 4.51g	9%
Vitamin A 12223.31IU	244
Vitamin C 30.83mg	51%

Cucumber Salad
in Miso Orange Sauce
serves 2

| 1 | large cucumber |
| | sea salt |

Sauce

	juice of one orange
1 TB	sweet white miso
1 TB	umeboshi paste or pulp of 2 plums
1 TB	ginger juice
2 drops	stevia clear liquid

1   Cut a 1/3 inch slice off one end of the cucumber and rub both ends together in a circular motion. This will bring any bitter foam to the surface. Wash off and repeat with the other side.

2   Slice cucumber in half then slice into thin half moons. It is not necessary to peel if organic.

3   Place cucumbers in a bowl, sprinkle sea salt liberally. Press out the liquid by placing a heavy object on top of the cucumbers for 30 minutes (such as another bowl filled with water or a plate with a rock on top). Drain off the water in a colander.

4   Combine sauce ingredients. Add to the cucumbers.

5   Allow cucumbers to marinate for 30 minutes or more.

Nutrition Facts — 1 Serving	
Calories 43.56 **% Daily Value**	
Total Fat 0.620g	0%
Saturated Fat 0.12g	0%
Cholesterol 0.00mg	0%
Sodium 1266.89mg	52%
Potassium 304.00mg	8%
Carbohydrates 8.65g	2%
Dietary Fiber 1.44g	5%
Protein 1.71g	3%
Vitamin C 19.89mg	33%

Cooking Tips
Scooping out the seeds will reduce any allergic reactions.

Celery Root and Mint Salad Roll Up

serves 4

Celery root is used widely in Europe in soups, salads and stir-fries. It is high in silicon and is used to treat high blood pressure. The toasted nori adds flavor, texture, color and many essential minerals and it's fun to eat.

1 cup	celery root, peeled and grated
1/2 cup	sunchokes (Jerusalem artichokes) scrubbed but not peeled, and grated
1/2	tart apple, grated
1/4 cup	mint leaves, finely chopped
3 stalks	green onions, thinly sliced diagonally

Dressing – combined in a cup

2 to 3 TB	coconut oil
1/4 cup or more	lemon juice
3 to 5 drops	stevia clear liquid
	sea salt to taste

1   In a bowl, blend the dressing and salad ingredients.
2   Allow flavors to combine for 30 minutes. Adjust to taste.
3   Place a few tablespoons in a sheet of toasted nori and roll.

Cooking Tips
This salad can also be rolled in red or green leaf lettuce or steamed cabbage leaves.

Nutrition Facts – 1 Serving	
Calories 168.35	**% Daily Value**
Total Fat 10.49g	16%
Saturated Fat 1.45g	7%
Cholesterol 0.00mg	0%
Sodium 173.78mg	7%
Potassium 541.42mg	15%
Carbohydrates 19.28g	6%
Dietary Fiber 7.70g	30%
Protein 1.75g	3%
Vitamin C 39.98mg	66%

Carrot Apple Slaw
serves 2

1 large	carrot, hand grated on large grate
1 small	apple, grated same as carrots
2 or 3	green onions, sliced diagonally
1/4 tsp.	cumin
1 TB	roasted sunflower seeds or roasted chopped walnuts

Orange Coconut Dressing (pg. 87)

1   Combine all ingredients in a bowl and blend in Orange Coconut Dressing.

Nutrition Facts – 1 Serving

Calories 111.67 **% Daily Value**

Total Fat 6.33g	9%
Saturated Fat 0.67g	3%
Cholesterol 0.00mg	0%
Sodium 22.51mg	0%
Potassium 309.29mg	8%
Carbohydrates 13.22g	4%
Dietary Fiber 4.05g	16%
Protein 2.78g	5%
Vitamin A 15549.011U	310%

SAUCES,
DRESSINGS
AND
CHUTNEYS

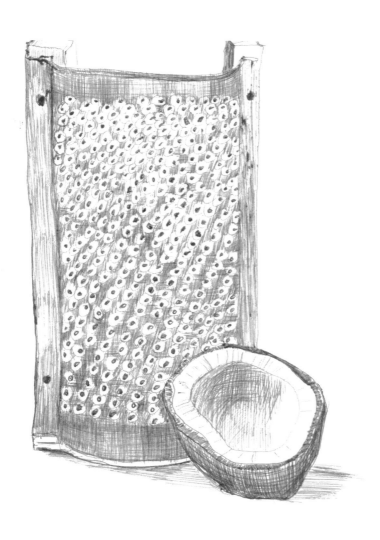

SAUCES, DRESSINGS AND CHUTNEYS

Coconut Tahini Sauce
serves 6/yields 1 1/2 cups

Serve with raw or cooked vegetables, pasta, noodles, grains, or on bread.

1 cup	coconut cream
1/3 to 1/2 cup	spring water, for desired consistency
1 to 2 TB	sweet onion, grated
1 TB	umeboshi paste, or 2 to 4 TB lemon juice
1 TB	sesame tahini
1 tsp.	coconut spread
	juice of half lemon
4 to 6 drops	stevia clear liquid

1   Combine all ingredients in a food processor or blender. Adjust seasonings to taste.

Nutrition Facts – 1 Serving	
Calories 152.87 **% Daily Value**	
Total Fat 15.51g	23%
Saturated Fat 12.85g	64%
Cholesterol 0.00mg	0%
Sodium 317.58mg	13%
Potassium 155.76mg	4%
Carbohydrates 4.11g	1%
Dietary Fiber 1.22g	4%
Protein 2.00g	4%

Basic Salad Dressing
serves 6

1/2 cup	coconut oil
1/3 cup	lemon juice
5 to 8 drops	stevia clear liquid, or to taste
	few pinches sea salt

1   Combine all ingredients.

Coconut Sour Cream
serves 4

Serve as a dip for raw vegetables and fruit, or on bread.

4 TB	coconut cream
4 TB	lemon juice
2 TB	sesame tahini
2 TB	coconut spread
4 drops	stevia clear liquid

1   Combine all ingredients in a bowl. Use the back of a soup spoon to blend the tahini and coconut spread. Adjust to taste.

Cranberry Apple Sauce
serves 4

You don't have to wait until Thanksgiving to enjoy this.

2 cups	spring water
1/2 lb.	cranberries, fresh or frozen
1 medium	apple, diced
3 to 5 drops	stevia concentrate or stevia clear liquid
pinch	sea salt
1 or 2 TB	coconut flakes

1   Rinse the berries and remove any stems. Place all ingredients in a pot, except the coconut flakes, and simmer until the berries have popped and the sauce has thickened to your preferred consistency. Add more spring water if necessary.
2   Sauce takes about 20 minutes to prepare or longer if you prefer a thicker sauce. Keep in mind that it will thicken when cooled.
3   Stir in the coconut flakes and add more sweetener if desired. Allow to cool before serving.

Nutrition Facts – 1 Serving	
Calories 33.83 **% Daily Value**	
Total Fat 0.18g	0%
Saturated Fat 0.02g	0%
Cholesterol 0.00mg	0%
Sodium 3.83mg	0%
Potassium 59.20mg	1%
Carbohydrates 8.75g	2%
Dietary Fiber 2.09g	8%
Protein 0.17g	0%

Coriander Chutney

serves 8/yields 2 cups

1/4 cup	lemon juice
1/4 cup	coconut water or spring water
1/4 lb.	cilantro - stems and leaves thoroughly washed and coarsely chopped, about 2 cups tightly packed
1/4 cup	coconut flakes
1/4 cup	onions, finely diced
2 TB	ginger root, peeled and minced
2 pinches	cayenne pepper, or to taste
	sea salt to taste

1   Purée lemon juice, coconut water or spring water and 1/2 cup cilantro in a blender or food processor. Scrape the sides and add another 1/2 cup cilantro. Blend for 30 seconds. Repeat until all cilantro is puréed.

2   Add the coconut flakes, onion, ginger, cayenne and salt and blend until the mixture is smooth.

3   Transfer to a bowl. Adjust seasonings to taste. Serve immediately.

Nutrition Facts – 1 Serving	
Calories 102.67	**% Daily Value**
Total Fat 9.24g	14%
Saturated Fat 8.13g	40%
Cholesterol 0.00mg	0%
Sodium 19.76mg	0%
Potassium 178.47mg	5%
Carbohydrates 5.57g	1%
Dietary Fiber 2.87g	11%
Protein 1.38g	2%

Date and Lemon Chutney
serves 8/yields 1 1/2 cups

8 oz.	Medjool dates, pitted and cut into 4 sections
1/4 cup	coconut flakes
1/4 cup	lemon juice
2 TB	ginger root, peeled and minced
1 TB	cilantro, minced
1/2 tsp.	fennel seeds
	sea salt to taste

1   In a serving bowl, combine dates, lemon juice, coconut, ginger and cilantro and toss with a spoon until well mixed.
2   Bruise the fennel seeds slightly by rubbing them briskly between your palms, then stir into the date mixture. Add sea salt and adjust seasonings to taste.
3   Serve at once.

Nutrition Facts – 1 Serving	
Calories 128.26 **% Daily Value**	
Total Fat 4.73g	7%
Saturated Fat 4.11g	20%
Cholesterol 0.00mg	0%
Sodium 4.18mg	0%
Potassium 244.18mg	6%
Carbohydrates 23.55g	7%
Dietary Fiber 3.41g	13%
Protein 1.13g	2%

Garlic Coconut Butter
yields 4 cups

This must be refrigerated otherwise bacteria will form. If you want to liquefy the oil, either let it sit for a while on the counter or place it in a bowl of hot water.

1/2 cup   peeled garlic cloves
4 cups   coconut oil

1   Purée the garlic cloves in a
blender with 1 cup of the oil.
Stir this paste into the remaining oil. Put in a glass bottle or
jar and refrigerate. In a few
days the oil will be ready and
will keep up to 3 weeks.

Nutrition Facts – 1 Serving	
Calories 119.03 **% Daily Value**	
Total Fat 13.63g	20%
Saturated Fat 11.79g	58%
Cholesterol 0.00mg	0%
Sodium 0.18mg	0%
Potassium 4.26mg	0%
Carbohydrates 0.35g	0%
Dietary Fiber 0.02g	0%
Protein 0.07g	0%

Orange Sesame Sauce
yields 1/4 cup

This tangy, sweet sauce is spectacular over vegetables,
sea vegetables, noodles, grain or whatever you can imag-
ine.

1/4 cup   freshly squeezed orange juice
2 TB   sesame tahini
1 TB   umeboshi paste, or 2 TB lemon juice
2 or more drops   stevia clear liquid

1   Whisk all ingredients in a
bowl, or use the back of a spoon
to blend tahini and umeboshi.

Nutrition Facts – 1 Serving	
Calories 198.90 **% Daily Value**	
Total Fat 14.52g	22%
Saturated Fat 2.03g	10%
Cholesterol 0.00mg	0%
Sodium 1902.82mg	79%
Potassium 248.20mg	7%
Carbohydrates 14.31g	4%
Dietary Fiber 2.91g	11%
Protein 5.78g	11%
Vitamin C 31.00mg	51%
Thiamin 0.44mg	29%

Savory Coconut and Banana

yields about a cup

Serve as an accompaniment to rice, over fruit, or enjoy it alone.

1 TB	coconut oil
1 tsp.	black mustard seeds
1 cup	coconut milk
1 TB	coconut flakes
pinch	sea salt, or to taste
1 medium	banana, ripe but firm, peeled and cut into 1/4-inch thick rounds
1 tsp.	mint leaves, minced

1   In a small, heavy skillet, heat oil over medium heat. Add mustard seeds. Sauté until they pop and become fragrant. Remove from heat. Add 2 TB of the coconut milk and the coconut flakes.

2   Place remaining coconut milk in a small bowl, stir in skillet mixture and sea salt. Add banana and mint and gently toss ingredients. Taste for seasoning. Cover and refrigerate 1 hour.

3   Will keep for up to one week in a sealed container.

Nutrition Facts – 1 Serving	
Calories 266.24	**% Daily Value**
Total Fat 25.49g	39%
Saturated Fat 22.46g	112%
Cholesterol 0.00mg	0%
Sodium 74.07mg	3%
Potassium 323.48mg	9%
Carbohydrates 11.35g	3%
Dietary Fiber 2.33g	9%
Protein 2.61g	5%

Tofu Basil Sauce
serves 6/yields 1 1/2 cups

This versatile sauce can be prepared to the consistency suitable for a raw vegetable dip, as a sauce over cooked vegetables, grains, noodles or pasta.

8 oz.	soft tofu
2 TB	sesame tahini
2 TB	sweet white miso
2 to 3 TB	balsamic vinegar
1/4-1/2 cup	spring water
1/4 cup	fresh basil, chopped
3 to 6 drops	stevia clear liquid

1   Mash tofu with a fork and combine with all of the ingredients, except stevia, in a blender. Blend until smooth.
2   Transfer to a bowl and add stevia to taste.

Cooking Tips
Suggestions: Substitute fresh mint leaves or dill for basil. Add raw or sautéed minced garlic cloves, cumin, curry, roasted caraway seeds or ginger juice.

Nutrition Facts – 1 Serving	
Calories 57.90 **% Daily Value**	
Total Fat 3.60g	5%
Saturated Fat 0.50g	2%
Cholesterol 0.00mg	0%
Sodium 179.51mg	7%
Potassium 102.21mg	2%
Carbohydrates 4.01g	1%
Dietary Fiber 0.82g	3%
Protein 3.10g	6%

Orange Coconut Dressing
yields 1/4 cup

Serve over cooked or raw vegetables, sea vegetables, grains, noodles or pasta.

1/4 cup	fresh squeezed orange juice
2 TB	coconut spread
1 TB	umeboshi paste or 2 TB lemon juice
pinch	ground cloves
2 or more drops	stevia clear liquid

1   Blend all ingredients in a bowl. It is easier to begin blending the coconut spread by starting with a small amount of orange juice and gradually adding more liquid until it's blended, then adding the remaining ingredients.

Nutrition Facts – 1 Serving	
Calories 126.90 **% Daily Value**	
Total Fat 10.53g	16%
Saturated Fat 9.24g	46%
Cholesterol 0.00mg	0%
Sodium 1881.82mg	78%
Potassium 221.50mg	6%
Carbohydrates 8.44g	2%
Dietary Fiber 0.78g	3%
Protein 1.52g	3%
Vitamin C 31.84mg	53%

COCONUT CUISINE 88

VEGETABLE DISHES

☼ VEGETABLE DISHES

Fennel and Collard Greens with Fennel Dressing

serves 4

Fennel Dressing also gives a wonderful flavor to any steamed vegetable.

2	fennel bulbs
1	bunch collard greens
1/4 cup	coconut oil
1	clove garlic
2 TB	coconut oil
pinch	grated nutmeg
	sea salt

Fennel Dressing

1   Cut the feathery fronds from the tops of the fennel bulbs. Chop these with the garlic. Place in a small bowl and mix with 1/4 cup coconut oil, grated nutmeg and a pinch of sea salt.

Nutrition Facts – 1 Serving	
Calories 221.98 **% Daily Value**	
Total Fat 20.56g	31%
Saturated Fat 2.74g	13%
Cholesterol 0.00mg	0%
Sodium 205.60mg	8%
Potassium 518.31mg	14%
Carbohydrates 9.84g	3%
Dietary Fiber 4.29g	17%
Protein 1.95g	3%
Vitamin C 20.67mg	34%

Collard Greens

1   Wash collard greens. Steam until tender. Remove to a cutting board, stack them and cut diago-nally and horizontally into bite-size pieces. Combine with the fennel seasoning. Place in the center of a serving plate.

Steamed Fennel Bulbs

1   Steam the fennel bulbs until just barely tender.
2   Cut lengthwise into quarters. Arrange the fennel pieces around the collard greens, and drizzle the remaining coconut oil over the fennel.

Curried Vegetables
serves 4 to 6

This is a basic recipe. Substitute other vegetables using the same procedure and curry ingredients. Serve with sautéed leafy green vegetables for a colorful and balanced meal.

1 TB	coconut oil
1 TB	yellow mustard seeds
1 large	onion, cut into cubes
1	yam, scrubbed and cubed - do not peel if organic
2	parsnips, peeled and cubed
1 cup	coconut cream
1/2 cup	Stevia GingerLemonade (pg. 28)
1/2 to 1 tsp.	curry powder
1/2 tsp.	turmeric
1/2 tsp.	sea salt

1   Heat a wok or heavy skillet until hot. Add the oil and swish it around the pan. Add the mustard seeds and when they begin to pop, cover the pan. When they have all popped, about 30 seconds, add the vegetables and condiments and quickly coat with the seeds.

Nutrition Facts – 1 Serving	
Calories 318.58 **% Daily Value**	
Total Fat 20.47g	31%
Saturated Fat 17.23g	86%
Cholesterol 0.00mg	0%
Sodium 204.32mg	8%
Potassium 863.61mg	24%
Carbohydrates 33.92g	11%
Dietary Fiber 8.40g	33%
Protein 4.37g	8%
Vitamin C 26.34mg	43%

2   Add the Stevia GingerLemonade and coconut cream, wait until it comes to a boil, reduce heat to medium low, cover and cook for 15 to 20 minutes or until the vegetables are soft.
3   Can be served over grains or noodles.

Cooking Tips
The vegetables should amount to about 4 cups. Cut them into equal sizes so that they will all cook evenly.

Heavenly Jerusalem Artichoke Purée

serves 4

Also known as sunchoke, this comfort food looks and feels like mashed potatoes. It has no relationship to the artichoke, but is a relative of the sunflower with a nutty-like flesh and a sweet and crunchy taste sweet. It provides a good source of potassium and vitamin C.

1 lb.   sunchokes, scrubbed, not peeled and sliced thin
coconut oil to taste
sea salt to taste

1   Steam the sunchokes until soft. Place in a blender with enough cooking water to blend and purée until smooth.
2   Transfer to a bowl and add the remaining ingredients. Adjust to taste.

Cooking Tips

Choose firm sunchokes that are not moldy, soft or wrinkled. Some sunchokes will have dark brown skin while others will be light brown in color, like ginger.
Refrigerate unwashed in a plastic bag for up to 1 week.
Dip cut sunchokes into a lemon juice and water mixture to prevent discoloration. Refrigerate sun chokes this way up to several days.

Nutrition Facts – 1 Serving	
Calories 104.94 **% Daily Value**	
Total Fat 1.14g	1%
Saturated Fat 0.15g	0%
Cholesterol 0.00mg	0%
Sodium 75.50mg	3%
Potassium 536.25mg	15%
Carbohydrates 21.80g	7%
Dietary Fiber 2.00g	8%
Protein 2.50g	5%
Iron 4.25mg	25%

Pan Fried Zucchini
with Ginger Apple Dressing

serves 2

This sauce also compliments cooked tempeh and any grilled, sautéed or raw vegetables.

	coconut oil for sautéing
2	zucchini, sliced in half lengthwise
2 or more cloves	garlic, minced
pinch	sea salt

Ginger Apple Sauce

1/3	sweet apple such as Fuji or red delicious, cored and diced
2 TB	ginger juice or 2-inch piece ginger root, peeled and diced
1/4 cup	sweet onion, diced
1/4 tsp. or to taste	sea salt
1 TB	coconut oil
3 TB	apple cider vinegar
1 TB	lemon juice
2 drops	stevia clear liquid

1   Rub sea salt on the zucchini. Heat a skillet, add the oil and heat. Sauté garlic for 1 minute. Add the zucchini slices face down, cover and cook on medium low heat for about 5 minutes until browned. Turn over and cook for a couple of minutes just until tender, but still firm.

Nutrition Facts – 1 Serving	
Calories 145.43 **% Daily Value**	
Total Fat 9.50g	14%
Saturated Fat 1.36g	6%
Cholesterol 0.00mg	0%
Sodium 652.10mg	27%
Potassium 642.19mg	18%
Carbohydrates 14.82g	4%
Dietary Fiber 3.53g	14%
Protein 3.82g	7%
Vitamin C 25.25mg	42%

Sauce

1   Combine ingredients in a food processor or blender. Adjust to taste.
2   Spread on top of the zucchini.

Sautéed Roots

serves 4

The sweetness of root vegetables is ever so comforting and safely satisfies the sweet craving.

1 TB	coconut oil
2 large	leeks, well cleaned and cut in thick diagonal slices
3 medium	carrots, scrubbed and roll cut or cut in thick diagonals
3 medium	parsnips, peeled and roll cut or cut in thick diagonals
	shoyu or tamari
1/2 cup	Stevia GingerLemonade or Marinade (pg. 28)
2 TB	roasted black or brown sesame seeds

1 In a large wok or skillet, heat oil and add leeks. Sauté on high heat for 1 minute, stirring constantly with a spatula to prevent sticking.

2 Add the remaining vegetables, a dash of shoyu or tamari and just enough stevia liquid to prevent the vegetables from burning (about 1/3 cup). Sauté quickly on a high heat for one minute, stirring constantly. Cover and cook on a medium-low flame.

3 Continue adding stevia liquid whenever necessary. Just before the vegetables are done, add a few more splashes of shoyu or tamari. It will take about 20 minutes or more until the vegetables are soft (depending on how thick their cut is).

4   Place vegetables in a serving bowl and sprinkle with roasted sesame seeds.

Cooking Tips

Add as little liquid as possible. This allows the vegetables to cook in their own juices producing a sweeter, more mellow taste.

Any root vegetables can be substituted. Try onions instead of leeks, or my favorite, lotus root.

Nutrition Facts – 1 Serving	
Calories 261.96 **% Daily Value**	
Total Fat 6.49g	9%
Saturated Fat 0.93g	4%
Cholesterol 0.00mg	0%
Sodium 302.02mg	12%
Potassium 1057.56mg	30%
Carbohydrates 49.78g	16%
Dietary Fiber 13.00g	51%
Protein 4.97g	9%
Vitamin A 17104.68IU	342%
Vitamin C 45.02mg	75%
Folate 175.95µg	43%
Magnesium 97.23mg	25%

Sweet Potato Purée

serves 2

This simple dish can be served with the main course or turned into aspic with agar-agar.

1	large sweet potato
1/2 to 1 cup	coconut milk or diluted with spring water
	juice of half lemon or 1 lime
1/2 tsp.	cumin powder
	pinch of nutmeg or cloves
1 drop	stevia clear liquid, or dusting of extract
	sea salt to taste

1   Wash and scrub the potato skin. Cut into slices. Steam until tender. Combine with the rest of the ingredients in a blender and blend until smooth. Adjust seasonings to taste.

Cooking Tips

The more liquid you add, the creamier the consistency.

Nutrition Facts – 1 Serving	
Calories 112.86 **% Daily Value**	
Total Fat 1.31g	2%
Saturated Fat 0.16g	0%
Cholesterol 0.00mg	0%
Sodium 24.00mg	1%
Potassium 715.12mg	20%
Carbohydrates 23.41g	7%
Dietary Fiber 3.93g	15%
Protein 2.90g	5%
Vitamin C 17.33mg	28%

Turkish Summer Squash with Coconut Yogurt Sauce

serves 4/yields 1 cup

This popular Turkish dish is traditionally prepared with home-made yogurt. This is a re-invented version.

Coconut Yogurt Sauce

1/2 cup	coconut cream
1/4 tsp.	ground cumin
3 TB	lemon juice
2 or more drops	stevia clear liquid

Dip

1 TB	coconut oil
1 cup	summer squash, cut into medium thick rounds
1 1/2 TB	tahini, well blended
1 small	garlic clove, crushed with 3 pinches of sea salt
1 tsp.	lemon juice
	sea salt to taste

1   Combine Coconut Yogurt Sauce ingredients in a small bowl.
2   In a small skillet, heat the oil and sauté the squash over medium-low heat until all moisture evaporates. With a slotted spoon press out the oil and discard. Leave the squash to cool to room temperature.

Nutrition Facts – 1 Serving	
Calories 168.38	**% Daily Value**
Total Fat 16.58g	25%
Saturated Fat 12.56g	62%
Cholesterol 0.00mg	0%
Sodium 6.64mg	0%
Potassium 215.77mg	6%
Carbohydrates 5.52g	1%
Dietary Fiber 1.62g	6%
Protein 2.52g	5%

3   Place the tahini, garlic and lemon juice in a mixing bowl and blend until smooth. Gradually fold in the Coconut Yogurt Sauce and then the squash. Add sea salt to taste.
4   Place in a shallow serving dish and allow to mellow at least 1 hour. Serve at room temperature with a sprinkling of ground cumin.

Vegetable Wrap with Guacamole
serves 4

1	onion, cut in half moons
1	red bell pepper
1	yellow bell pepper
1	green bell pepper
1 clove	garlic, minced
8 oz.	button mushrooms
3 TB	coconut oil
2 TB	chili powder
	sea salt to taste

Guacamole

1 ripe	avocado, mashed
1	shallot, coarsely chopped
1 fresh	green chili, seeded and coarsely chopped
2 drops	stevia clear liquid
	juice of 1 lime
	sea salt to taste

To serve

4 to 6	whole wheat wraps, pita bread, or steamed red cabbage leaves

1   Cut the peppers in half, remove the seeds and cut the flesh into strips. Combine the onion and peppers in a bowl. Add the crushed garlic and mix lightly.

2   Remove the mushroom stalks and discard. Slice the mushroom caps and add to the pepper mixture in the bowl. Mix the oil and chili powder in a cup, pour over vegetables and stir well. Set aside.

3   Make the guacamole: Put the flesh into a food processor or blender with the rest of the ingredients; or blend with a fork.

4   Process for 1 minute, until smooth. Scrape into a small bowl, cover tightly and refrigerate.

5   Heat a skillet or wok until very hot. Add the marinated vegetables and stir-fry over high heat for 5 to 6 minutes, until the mushrooms and peppers are just tender. Season with salt. Spoon the filling onto each wrap or cabbage leaf and roll, or fill pita pockets.

6   Serve with the guacamole.

Nutrition Facts – 1 Serving		
Calories 475.71	**% Daily Value**	
Total Fat 20.56g		31%
Saturated Fat 10.40g		52%
Cholesterol 0.00mg		0%
Sodium 400.99mg		16%
Potassium 1270.30mg		36%
Carbohydrates 69.43g		23%
Dietary Fiber 11.17g		44%
Protein 13.23g		26%
Vitamin A 5160.55IU		103%
Vitamin C 203.66mg		339%
Iron 5.40mg		29%
Thiamin 0.46mg		30%
Riboflavin 0.43mg		25%
Niacin 6.26mg		31%
Vitamin B6 1.05mg		52%
Folate 129.00µg		32%
Phosphorus 298.13mg		29%
Magnesium 110.62mg		27%

Sautéed String Beans and Garlic

serves 4

1/2 lb.	string beans
1 or more TB	coconut oil
2 or 3 large	garlic cloves, thinly sliced
	sea salt to taste

1   Cut off the root end of the string beans. Steam with the lid slightly ajar until the beans are crisp, about 5 minutes. Transfer the beans immediately to a bowl.

2   Heat a large skillet, add the oil and then the garlic and salt. Sauté for a couple of minutes. Don't let the garlic burn. Turn off the heat and blend in the beans.

Nutrition Facts – 1 Serving		
Calories 50.80	**% Daily Value**	
Total Fat 3.48g		5%
Saturated Fat 2.96g		14%
Cholesterol 0.00mg		0%
Sodium 3.85mg		0%
Potassium 129.03mg		3%
Carbohydrates 4.92g		1%
Dietary Fiber 1.98g		7%
Protein 1.20g		2%

Dandelion Greens With Crispy Onions
serves 3

This can be a vegetable accompaniment or a main dish for lunch. Other winter greens such as escarole, kale, mustard greens, Swiss chard or spinach can be prepared in the same way.

3 TB	coconut oil
2 medium	onions, peeled and thinly sliced
1 1/2 lb.	dandelion greens, washed and stemmed
pinch	course sea salt
1 clove	garlic, peeled and crushed with sea salt
2 TB	lemon juice
	sea salt to taste
4	lemon wedges for garnish
2	sliced radishes

1   Heat oil in a large, heavy skillet. Pat the onions dry between paper towels. Add the onions to the skillet; cook over medium low heat stirring often until golden, about 10 minutes.

2   Remove half the onions with a slotted spoon and set them aside to cool.

3   Increase the heat and continue cooking the remaining onions, until crisp and golden brown, about 5 minutes. Transfer the fried onions with a slotted spoon to a paper towel to drain.

4   Blanch or steam the greens with the sea salt until just tender. Remove to a cutting board and slice into even sections.

5   Place the greens and the reserved golden-stage onions in the skillet, add the garlic and cook until thick and soft to the bite, about 5 minutes, stirring often.

6   Stir in the lemon juice and add more salt, if desired.

7   Serve warm, sprinkled with the crisp onions and surrounded with lemon wedges and radishes.

Nutrition Facts – 1 Serving	
Calories 198.14 **% Daily Value**	
Total Fat 14.15g	21%
Saturated Fat 11.88g	59%
Cholesterol 0.00mg	0%
Sodium 328.77mg	13%
Potassium 475.26mg	13%
Carbohydrates 20.38g	6%
Dietary Fiber 3.87g	15%
Protein 2.88g	5%
Vitamin A 7718.28IU	154%
Vitamin C 67.14mg	111%

Lotus Root And Garlic Chives
serves 4

These vegetables are available at Oriental markets or on the Internet.

	coconut oil for sautéing
2 small links	fresh lotus root, peeled and sliced into thin rounds
1 cup	garlic chives, cut diagonally into 1-inch slices
1/2 cup	Stevia GingerLemonade, Stevia Marinade (pg. 29) or 3 drops stevia clear liquid in 1/2 cup spring water
	sea salt

1   In a heavy skillet or wok, heat oil and sauté the lotus root for 10 minutes on medium heat, adding just enough stevia liquid when necessary to prevent burning.

2 Cover and cook on medium heat until they soften, about 10 to 15 minutes (depending on their thickness). Add the salt and chives a few minutes before the end of cooking. Add more liquid whenever needed.

Nutrition Facts – 1 Serving	
Calories 67.70 **% Daily Value**	
Total Fat 3.53g	5%
Saturated Fat 0.51g	2%
Cholesterol 0.00mg	0%
Sodium 159.76mg	6%
Potassium 291.28mg	8%
Carbohydrates 8.45g	2%
Dietary Fiber 2.55g	10%
Protein 1.59g	3%
Vitamin C 27.21mg	45%

Stir-Fried Baby Bok Choy
serves 4

This is a simple and tasty accompaniment to any main course.

Nutrition Facts – 1 Serving	
Calories 87.37 **% Daily Value**	
Total Fat 7.18g	11%
Saturated Fat 5.97g	29%
Cholesterol 0.00mg	0%
Sodium 56.25mg	2%
Potassium 525.00mg	15%
Carbohydrates 5.88g	1%
Dietary Fiber 5.00g	20%
Protein 2.13g	4%
Vitamin A 5000.00IU	100%
Vitamin C 30.00mg	50%
Folate 136.88µg	34%

1 lb.   baby bok choy
2 TB   coconut oil
2 TB   minced garlic or ginger
         tamari, shoyu or sea salt

1 Wash and trim the baby bok choy. Remove any discolored leaves and damaged stems.
2 Heat a wok or heavy skillet until very hot, add the oil and swirl it around. Sauté garlic or ginger for 1 or 2 minutes.
3 Add the baby bok choy, sprinkle with your choice of salt seasoning and stir-fry for 2 to 3 minutes, until the greens have wilted a little, but are still crisp.
4 Serve immediately.

Cooking Tips
This green can be replaced with the larger sized variety of bok choy or choy sam, the flowering Chinese cabbage.

Sweet Vegetables in Peanut & Coconut Sauce

serves 4

This is really good!

1 medium	sweet potato, diced and steamed
1 large	onion, diced or cut in half moons
1 large	ear of corn, kernels removed
1 TB	coconut oil
2 large	garlic cloves
1-inch piece	ginger root, peeled and finely sliced
1/4 tsp.	sea salt

Sauce

1/3 cup	peanut butter
1 1/2 to 2 cups	coconut milk
juice of 1 lime	
1 tsp.	coriander powder
1/2 tsp.	curry
1/2 tsp.	Garam masala powder (optional)
dash	red pepper flakes

1   Combine sauce ingredients in a bowl.

2   Heat a wok or skillet and add oil. Sauté garlic and ginger for one minute. Add the onions and sea salt and sauté until translucent.

3   Add the sauce ingredients and cook for 5 minutes. Add the corn kernels and sweet potatoes and cook for 2 minutes.

4   Serve over basmati or long grain rice.

Nutrition Facts – 1 Serving	
Calories 405.63 **% Daily Value**	
Total Fat 32.84g	50%
Saturated Fat 18.68g	93%
Cholesterol 0.00mg	0%
Sodium 143.34mg	5%
Potassium 579.15mg	16%
Carbohydrates 25.65g	8%
Dietary Fiber 4.07g	16%
Protein 9.11g	18%
Vitamin A 6623.78IU	132%
Vitamin C 14.39mg	25%
Iron 3.76mg	25%

COCONUT CUISINE 104

GRAINS, BEANS
AND NOODLES

GRAINS, BEANS AND NOODLES

Couscous and Garbanzo Bean Salad

serves 4

1 cup	spring water
1 cup	couscous
pinch	sea salt
12 oz. can	garbanzo beans
1 medium	carrot, diced
2 stalks	celery, diced
1/2 cup	sweet or red onion, diced
1/2 cup	fresh mint leaves or cilantro, minced
2 TB	roasted black sesame seeds
	coconut flakes for garnish

Dressing – combined in a cup

3 TB	coconut oil
2 TB	apple cider or balsamic vinegar
1/3 cup	lemon juice
3 to 5 drops	stevia clear liquid
	sea salt to taste

1   Boil water. Stir in couscous and salt. Remove from heat and cover. Allow 5 minutes for grains to absorb water. Gently fluff with a fork or rice paddle.

2   In a small saucepan, blanch carrots in 1/2-cup spring water or Stevia Marinade for 2 minutes. Drain.

3   In a large serving bowl, combine all ingredients and gently fold in dressing.

4   Allow flavors to combine for 30 minutes. Readjust taste before serving.

5   Sprinkle some coconut flakes on each individual serving. Serve at room temperature.

Nutrition Facts – 1 Serving	
Calories 276.25	**% Daily Value**
Total Fat 11.54g	17%
Saturated Fat 1.60g	7%
Cholesterol 0.00mg	0%
Sodium 211.07mg	8%
Potassium 432.27mg	12%
Carbohydrates 36.96g	12%
Dietary Fiber 6.85g	27%
Protein 8.41g	16%
Vitamin A 6097.49IU	121%
Vitamin C 17.79	29%

Blackened Tofu Cutlets

serves 6

I used a coffee substitute made from roasted soybeans as the blackening ingredient, although ground coffee beans can also be used. Serve as a side dish or cut into small cubes and add to salads or stir-fries.

16 oz.	extra firm tofu
6 TB	coffee substitute crystals or ground coffee
6 TB	coconut oil
3 TB	tamari
1/2 tsp	freshly ground black pepper

1   Cut tofu block in half widthwise. Cut each half into thirds, lengthwise.

2   Blend the rest of the ingredients in a bowl. Marinate tofu slices in mixture for 10 minutes.

3   Place the slices in a heated skillet. Fry each side on medium heat until crispy. Be sure each slice fits comfortably in the skillet to ensure even cooking.

Nutrition Facts – 1 Serving	
Calories 201.05 **% Daily Value**	
Total Fat 18.32g	28%
Saturated Fat 12.45g	62%
Cholesterol 0.00mg	0%
Sodium 1013.12mg	42%
Potassium 140.91mg	4%
Carbohydrates 2.60g	0%
Dietary Fiber 0.49g	1%
Protein 9.78g	19%

Barley Salad
serves 6

Pearl barley is an easily digestible grain. It has a cooling effect on the body and a sweet and salty flavor. Presentation is also part of the eating experience and this salad has great eye-appeal.

1 cup	pearl barley, washed and cooked in 2 cups spring water
1 large	carrot, diced
1 cup	sweet or red onion, diced
1	yellow, orange or red bell pepper, diced
1/2 cup	fennel or celery, diced
1/4 cup	roasted sunflower seeds
1/4 cup	fresh dill, parsley or cilantro, minced
1/4 cup	fresh mint, minced

Dressing

3 or 4 TB	coconut oil
1/4 cup	lemon juice
1/4 tsp.	cumin powder
4 or more drops	stevia clear liquid
	sea salt to taste

1   Transfer cooked barley to a large bowl to cool. Gently fluff with a rice paddle or chopsticks.

2   Combine dressing ingredients in a cup.

3   Either water sauté the carrots in 1/2 cup Stevia Marinade or spring water for a few minutes until tender but crisp; or sauté carrots in a little coconut oil with ginger slices or ginger juice and a hint of stevia extract, or a few drops of stevia clear liquid.

4   Combine barley with the rest of the ingredients, add the dressing and allow flavors to meld for 30 minutes in the refrigerator. Adjust seasonings - you may need to add more lemon juice before serving.

Cooking Tips

Barley cooks in about 40 to 50 minutes. For better digestibility, soak the barley for at least 4 hours before cooking. Cook with soaking water.

Nutrition Facts – 1 serving	
Calories 253.10 **% Daily Value**	
Total Fat 12.81g	19%
Saturated Fat 1.72g	8%
Cholesterol 0.00mg	0%
Sodium 103.53mg	4%
Potassium 276.37mg	7%
Carbohydrates 31.69g	10%
Dietary Fiber 7.03g	28%
Protein 5.25g	10%
Vitamin A 5352.96IU	107%
Vitamin C 49.83mg	83%

Pasta with Basil and Garlic
serves 2 to 4

8 oz.	spaghetti
4 TB	coconut oil
2 TB	garlic, thinly sliced
	sea salt to taste
2/3 cup	fresh basil, finely chopped

1   Cook spaghetti according to the package directions. Drain. Place in a large bowl.

2   Heat a heavy skillet, add the oil and heat. Add the garlic and salt. Sauté on medium heat until lightly brown. Stir in the basil.

3   Add the garlic mixture to the pasta and blend well. Add more oil and salt if desired.

Nutrition Facts – 1 Serving	
Calories 270.75 **% Daily Value**	
Total Fat 11.66g	17%
Saturated Fat 9.52g	47%
Cholesterol 0.00mg	0%
Sodium 4.13mg	0%
Potassium 116.83mg	3%
Carbohydrates 35.69g	11%
Dietary Fiber 1.40g	5%
Protein 6.24g	12%

Buckwheat Groats

serves 4

This dish is especially warming and nourishing on cold winter days. Buckwheat nourishes the lungs, kidneys and bladder and aids in eliminating water or fluid retention. It is a safe grain for those with wheat allergies. By adding some cooked pasta bows to this dish, it becomes a traditional Jewish favorite - kasha varnishkas.

	coconut oil for sautéing
1	onion, diced
pinch	sea salt
1/2 head	cabbage, cored and sliced fine or grated
3 drops	stevia clear liquid in 1/2 cup spring water
1 cup	roasted buckwheat groats
2 cups	boiling spring water
1 cup	parsley or cilantro, minced

1   Lightly brush a heavy skillet with coconut oil. Add onions and sea salt and sauté until translucent.

2   Add cabbage and just enough stevia water to prevent burning and sauté for 2 minutes. Add the buckwheat and sauté for 1 minute.

3   Add the boiling water, cover and simmer for 25 to 30 minutes until water is absorbed. Add the parsley or cilantro one minute before the end of cooking. Adjust salt to taste.

Nutrition Facts – 1 Serving	
Calories 69.85 **% Daily Value**	
Total Fat 2.64g	4%
Saturated Fat 0.39g	1%
Cholesterol 0.00mg	0%
Sodium 84.39mg	3%
Potassium 146.23mg	4%
Carbohydrates 10.76g	3%
Dietary Fiber 1.98g	7%
Protein 1.98g	3%

Coconut Wild Rice
serves 4 to 6

2 cups	wild rice
2 cups	spring water
2 1/2 cups	coconut milk
1/2 tsp.	sea salt
2 or 3 drops	stevia clear liquid
	coconut flakes for garnish

1   Wash the rice several times in cold water until it runs clear. Place all ingredients, except coconut flakes, in a heavy-bottomed saucepan.

2   Bring to a boil, cover and reduce heat to low. Simmer until all the water is absorbed and the rice is just beginning to stick to the bottom of the pot.

3   Turn off the heat and allow the rice to rest in the saucepan for about 5 to 10 minutes.

4   Gently fluff the rice with a rice paddle. Garnish each bowl with coconut flakes.

Nutrition Facts – 1 Serving	
Calories 375.91 **% Daily Value**	
Total Fat 20.66g	31%
Saturated Fat 17.89g	89%
Cholesterol 0.00mg	0%
Sodium 173.83mg	7%
Potassium 434.90mg	12%
Carbohydrates 42.59g	14%
Dietary Fiber 3.31g	13%
Protein 9.76g	19%
Iron 4.16mg	25%
Phosphorus 321.33mg	32%
Magnesium 138.11mg	34%
Zinc 3.72mg	25%

Marinated Tofu Kebabs

serves 4

8 oz.	extra firm tofu
Marinade	
4 TB	coconut oil
1 tsp.	tamari
3 to 5 cloves	garlic, minced
1 TB	ginger root, peeled and thinly sliced
5 to 7 drops	stevia clear liquid
3 cups	whole button mushrooms, zucchini and onions cut into chunks

1   Combine marinade ingredients in a large ceramic or glass bowl.
2   Cut tofu block into 1/2-inch cubes. Coat with the marinade and marinate for at least 1 hour.
3   Skewer tofu cubes, onions, mushrooms and zucchini and brush with marinade. Broil or grill until golden, turning occasionally.

Nutrition Facts – 1 Serving	
Calories 186.62 **% Daily Value**	
Total Fat 17.26g	26%
Saturated Fat 12.30g	61%
Cholesterol 0.00mg	0%
Sodium 92.44mg	3%
Potassium 315.46mg	9%
Carbohydrates 4.12g	1%
Dietary Fiber 1.38g	5%
Protein 7.17g	14%

Millet Croquettes

serves 6/yields about 12 croquettes

Millet is the most alkaline of all grains. It is high in protein and silicon and is known to strengthen the kidneys. One part millet cooked with six times water makes a delicious and strengthening morning porridge. Turn these croquettes into a loaf simply by placing ingredients in an oiled loaf pan to bake.

1 cup	millet, soaked overnight
2 1/2 cups	spring water
8 oz.	firm tofu
1 cup each	corn, sweet potatoes or yams, onions - diced
1 tsp.	coconut oil
2 TB	shoyu or tamari
1 tsp.	ground cumin
1/3 cup	Stevia Marinade or GingerLemonade (pg. 28)

1   Bring water and millet to a boil. Turn heat to low and cook for about 20 minutes or until water is absorbed. When finished, fluff with a fork or rice paddle, then transfer to a bowl.

2   Sauté the onions in oil and a pinch of sea salt until transparent. Add the rest of the vegetables, a pinch more sea salt and stir-fry for 2 minutes. Add the stevia liquid, cover and cook on medium heat until liquid has evaporated and the vegetables are tender.

3   Mash the tofu with your hands and blend with the millet. Add the vegetables, cumin and shoyu and mix together well.

4   Form into a firm ball with about 3 or 4 TB of the mixture, then gently flatten. Place croquettes on an oiled baking tray. Bake at 350 degrees for 30 to 40 minutes, depending on the size and thickness of your croquette, until brown and crispy on top.

5   Serve with any of the Sauces or with mustard.

Nutrition Facts – 1 Serving	
Calories 159.63	**% Daily Value**
Total Fat 3.16g	4%
Saturated Fat 0.47g	2%
Cholesterol 0.00mg	0%
Sodium 342.34mg	14%
Potassium 159.48mg	4%
Carbohydrates 26.59g	8%
Dietary Fiber 3.13g	12%
Protein 6.08g	12%

Cooking Tips

Ordinarily, millet is cooked with 3 times water. For this recipe, I have used less water in order to achieve a less moist result.

Vegan Singapore Noodles
serves 4

This hot and spicy dish can be tamed by eliminating the cayenne pepper and curry. Because hot spices have a cooling effect, this is usually eaten in the summer months. Traditionally, these noodles are made with shrimp. This is the vegan version.

Noodle Ingredients

1/4 lb.	thin vermicelli rice noodles, softened in hot water for about 15 minutes and drained
2 tsp.	coconut oil
1 1/2 tsp.	Madras curry powder
3 1/2 cups	finely shredded leeks or scallions
1 1/2 TB	minced fresh ginger root
3 cups	bean sprouts, rinsed and drained

Singapore Sauce

1/3 cup	spring water or vegetable broth
2 tsp.	coconut spread
3 drops	stevia clear liquid, or to taste
	sea salt to taste
pinch or two	cayenne pepper

1   Blend Singapore Sauce ingredients in a separate bowl.

2   Heat a wok or heavy skillet over high heat. Add oil and heat until hot. Add curry and stir-fry until fragrant. Add leeks and ginger and stir-fry for about 2 minutes. Add bean sprouts and cook for 20 seconds. Add rice noodles and Singapore Sauce and toss gently until the noodles have absorbed the sauce and are tender.

3   Transfer to a platter and serve.

Nutrition Facts – 1 Serving	
Calories 185.94 **% Daily Value**	
Total Fat 3.34g	5%
Saturated Fat 0.98g	4%
Cholesterol 0.00mg	0%
Sodium 577.12mg	24%
Potassium 203.58mg	5%
Carbohydrates 37.94g	12%
Dietary Fiber 1.92g	7%
Protein 2.97g	5%

Syrian White Bean Salad

serves 4

This is my version of a popular dish from northern Syria and Turkey. It's even better the next day.

16 oz. can	navy or canellini beans
2 TB	lemon juice
	sea salt to taste
pinch	freshly ground black pepper
3 TB	cilantro, finely chopped
2 stalks	scallions, thinly sliced diagonally
2 TB	walnuts, finely chopped
1 TB	coconut oil
3 pinches	Hungarian paprika
1 pinch	mildly hot red pepper flakes

1   Rinse the beans in a colander. In a saucepan, add beans, lemon juice and a pinch of sea salt. Heat until mildly hot. Remove to a glass or ceramic bowl. Toss well and let stand for 10 minutes.

2   Add remaining ingredients and toss again. Serve cold or at room temperature.

Nutrition Facts – 1 Serving	
Calories 185.61 **% Daily Value**	
Total Fat 6.44g	9%
Saturated Fat 3.32g	16%
Cholesterol 0.00mg	0%
Sodium 4.40mg	0%
Potassium 471.74mg	13%
Carbohydrates 24.98g	8%
Dietary Fiber 9.78g	39%
Protein 8.77g	17%

Fried Polenta
serves 6

Polenta also makes a nourishing breakfast porridge.

1 cup	course or medium course corn meal
4 cups	spring water
1 TB	coconut oil
	sea salt

1   Boil water separately. Dry roast corn meal in heavy pot on low heat until fragrant, stirring frequently. Add the boiling water slowly, stirring constantly to prevent lumping. Add sea salt and cook for 30 minutes or more, stirring occasionally, until it has a soft, gritty taste.

Nutrition Facts – 1 Serving

Calories 73.61	**% Daily Value**
Total Fat 0.73g	1%
Cholesterol 0.00mg	0%
Potassium 58.36mg	1%
Carbohydrates 15.63g	5%
Protein 0.00g	0%

2   Lightly oil a 2 quart mold and press the polenta into it, working out any air pockets.
3   Refrigerate until it firms. Unmold and slice.
4   Heat a skillet and add oil. When oil is hot, but not smoking, add the slices. Fry until crispy on both sides.
5   Serve with a sweet spread, or if you prefer it salty, serve with shoyu or tamari diluted with spring water.

Cooking Tips
Cut the fried polenta into small cubes and serve as croutons on soups or in salads.

Sweet and Sour Tempeh
serves 2

Tempeh is a fermented food made from soybeans. This digestible form of protein can be broiled, fried, braised, or sautéed, served in a sandwich with lettuce and cucumbers, or added to vegetable, pasta, or grain dishes.

1/2 lb.	tempeh cut into 1/4 x 2-inch strips

Marinade

	juice of 1/2 orange
1 to 2 TB	sweet white miso or brown rice miso, or 1 TB tamari
1 tsp	ginger juice
4 drops	stevia clear liquid

1   Marinate tempeh for 30 minutes.
2   Place tempeh and marinade in a skillet, cover and cook slowly for 15 minutes. If it needs more liquid, add a small amount of spring water or orange juice.

Nutrition Facts – 1 Serving	
Calories 278.06 **% Daily Value**	
Total Fat 14.80g	22%
Saturated Fat 4.20g	20%
Cholesterol 0.00mg	0%
Sodium 321.48mg	13%
Potassium 581.44mg	16%
Carbohydrates 17.38g	5%
Dietary Fiber 0.53g	2%
Protein 23.96g	47%
Vitamin C 15.55mg	25%
Phosphorus 334.54mg	33%
Magnesium 103.84mg	25%

Quinoa Tabouli
serves 4

Quinoa is a staple grain of South America. It has the highest protein and fat content of any grain. It is especially high in calcium and is a good source of B vitamins, vitamin E, iron and phosphorus. It must be washed very well to rinse off the bitterness from its surface.

1 cup	quinoa, rinsed well
1 3/4 cups	spring water
	pinch of sea salt
1 cup	minced parsley or cilantro
1	finely diced tomato or 3/4 cup quartered cherry tomatoes

Dressing

1/3 cup	lemon juice
2 or more TB	coconut oil
1 to 2 drops	stevia clear liquid
	sea salt to taste

1   Place quinoa and sea salt in water. Bring to a boil, cover, turn heat to low, and cook until all water is absorbed, about 15 minutes. Cool. Fluff with a fork.
2   Combine dressing ingredients in a cup.
3   In a large bowl, combine quinoa with the rest of the ingredients and add the dressing. Adjust to taste.

4   Allow flavors to meld for 30 minutes before serving. May need more lemon juice.

Cooking Tips
Stuff a portion of the tabouli inside a half red bell pepper for a colorful presentation, a refreshing taste and a crunchy texture.

Nutrition Facts – 1 serving	
Calories 291.84 **% Daily Value**	
Total Fat 16.13g	24%
Saturated Fat 2.09g	10%
Cholesterol 0.00mg	0%
Sodium 162.44mg	6%
Potassium 466.47mg	13%
Carbohydrates 32.62g	10%
Dietary Fiber 3.26g	13%
Protein 6.14g	12%
Vitamin C 17.31mg	28%
Iron 4.34mg	25%

Mung Bean Noodles with Orange Sesame Sauce

serves 2

These light and digestible noodles are sold in Oriental markets. They come packaged in individually wrapped portions. Best of all, they don't need to be cooked.

2 servings	mung bean noodles
	pot of boiled spring water
1 cup	green onions, diagonally sliced
1 cup	red bell peppers, thinly sliced

Orange Sesame Sauce (pg. 84)

1   Soak the noodles in enough water to cover for 15 minutes, until soft. Rinse and drain in a colander. With a scissors, cut strands into thirds and place in a serving bowl.
2   Add bell peppers, green onions and blend in Orange Sesame Sauce.

Nutrition Facts – 1 serving	
Calories 222.30 **% Daily Value**	
Total Fat 1.17g	1%
Saturated Fat 0.17g	0%
Cholesterol 0.00mg	0%
Sodium 15.88mg	0%
Potassium 282.63mg	8%
Carbohydrates 52.00g	17%
Dietary Fiber 3.21g	12%
Protein 1.99g	3%
Vitamin A 4440.26IU	88%
Vitamin C 150.95mg	251%

Rice Pilaf
serves 4

Brown rice is high in B vitamins and soothing on the stomach. The short grain variety has a chewier texture and is more suitable for cooler weather. Long grain as well as basmati is best for warm weather. The medium variety is for all seasons.

1 cup	basmati, long or medium grain brown rice
2 cups	spring water
1 TB	coconut oil
1 large	carrot, diced
1 medium	onion, diced
1/2 cup	fennel, diced
3 drops	stevia clear liquid
1/4 tsp.	sea salt
1/4 cup	roasted unhulled black or brown sesame seeds
3 stalks	green onions, sliced diagonally for garnish

1   Wash rice well until water runs clear, then drain. In a heavy skillet, dry roast the rice on a low heat, stirring gently until a nutty fragrance arises - about 7 minutes. Transfer rice to a bowl.
2   Boil water in a saucepan.
3   In a separate pot, heat oil. Add onion, fennel, carrot, stevia and salt and sauté on a high heat for 2 minutes. Stir in the rice. Add the boiling water, reduce flame to low, cover and cook until water is absorbed, about 45 minutes.
4   Transfer to a bowl and stir in the sesame seeds and green onions.

Cooking Tips

Dry roasting the rice gives it a nutty, light texture. For a different flavor, sauté minced garlic or slivered ginger with the vegetables or add your own spice and herb preferences such as cayenne, curry, turmeric or cumin.

Nutrition Facts – 1 serving	
Calories 315.30	**% Daily Value**
Total Fat 11.72g	18%
Saturated Fat 1.73g	8%
Cholesterol 0.00mg	0%
Sodium 135.85mg	5%
Potassium 391.68mg	11%
Carbohydrates 47.15g	15%
Dietary Fiber 5.75g	23%
Protein 7.35g	14%
Vitamin A 5792.14IU	115%

SNACKS

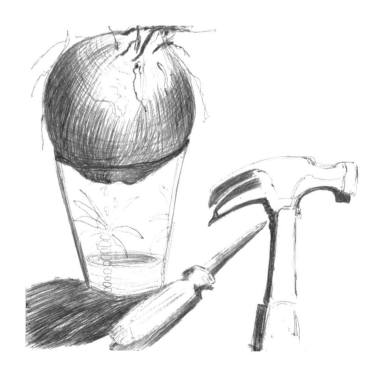

Coconut Popcorn

serves 4

1/2 cup	popping corn
2 or more TB	coconut oil

Stove Top Method

1 Heat a heavy pot. Add coconut oil and heat. Keep at medium high heat. Add popcorn, cover the pot and shake frequently to prevent burning until popped. Add sea salt or roasted dulse, if desired.

Nutrition Facts – 1 Serving	
Calories 82 **% Daily Value**	
Total Fat 7.05g	10%
Saturated Fat 5.92g	29%
Cholesterol 0.00mg	0%
Sodium 0.24mg	0%
Potassium 18.06mg	0%
Carbohydrates 4.67g	1%
Dietary Fiber 0.91g	3%
Protein 0.72g	1%

Roasted Dulse

Dulse seaweed is high in iodine and manganese with virtually no calories. Its salty flavor is similar to bacon making it a healthy substitute for a BLT sandwich. Eat as a snack; crumble in salads, soups, porridge; or sprinkle on grains or pasta. When soaked, it expands and can be used in salads.

Nutrition Facts – 1 Serving	
Calories 22.50 **% Daily Value**	
Total Fat 0g	0%
Saturated Fat 0.06g	0%
Cholesterol 0.00mg	0%
Sodium 436.00mg	12%
Potassium 547.00mg	16%
Carbohydrates 4.57g	1%
Dietary Fiber 0.25g	1%
Protein 1.51g	3%
Iodine	243%
Iron	25%
Vitamin B 6	42%
Vitamin B 12	26%
Folate 97.75µg	27%

1/3 cup	dulse

1 Toast in the oven at 200 degree F. until crispy, or dry roast in a skillet over a medium heat until crispy.
2 Dulse Chips: Pan fry in a well-oiled skillet until they turn brownish and crisp.

Cumin Roasted Sunflower Seeds
serves 4

Purchase them fresh to avoid rancidity. These are wonderful as a snack or added to any grain, pasta or vegetable dish.

1 cup sunflower seeds
       cumin powder

1 On a low flame, dry roast sunflower seeds in a 10-inch skillet. Shake the skillet frequently being careful not to burn them; their color should be golden brown. Add cumin and stir to blend. Remove from heat immediately.
Cooking time: 5 minutes

Nutrition Facts – 1 Serving	
Calories 208.35 **% Daily Value**	
Total Fat 19.09g	29%
Saturated Fat 2.00g	9%
Cholesterol 0.00mg	0%
Sodium 1.45mg	0%
Potassium 169.18mg	4%
Carbohydrates 7.01g	2%
Dietary Fiber 5.81g	11%
Phosphorus	38%

Roasted Sesame Seeds
serves 6/yields 1/2 cup

Both black and brown unhulled sesame seeds are high in calcium and vitamin E and benefit the liver and kidneys. Because they are high in oxalic acid, they should not be eaten raw. Soaking them overnight, then roasting will reduce the oxalic acid even more. Be careful not to burn them.

1/2 cup sesame seeds, unhulled

Nutrition Facts – 1 Serving	
Calories 68.76 **% Daily Value**	
Total Fat 5.96g	9%
Saturated Fat 0.83g	4%
Cholesterol 0.00mg	0%
Sodium 1.32mg	0%
Potassium 56.16mg	1%
Carbohydrates 2.81g	0%
Dietary Fiber 1.42g	5%
Protein 2.13g	4%

1 Place enough seeds to fit comfortably in a skillet. Dry roast on low heat. Shake the pan frequently to prevent burning. To test for doneness, moisten your index finger, gather some seeds on it, and taste to determine if they're crunchy. Transfer seeds immediately to a bowl.

Tamari Roasted Pumpkin Seeds
serves 8

Pumpkin seeds are known to benefit the male prostate gland. Roasting will make them more digestible, but be careful not to burn them. This will destroy the omega-3 fatty acids. Sprinkle them in salads, grain dishes, vegetable dishes, as a garnish for soups or just enjoy as a snack.

1 cup   pumpkin seeds
        splash of shoyu
        or tamari

1   Place enough seeds that fit comfortably in a skillet. Roast on a low flame shaking the pan frequently to prevent burning. When they begin to pop, add a couple of splashes of shoyu or tamari and coat evenly. Remove immediately from heat.

Nutrition Facts – 1 Serving	
Calories 148.57	**% Daily Value**
Total Fat 11.96g	18%
Saturated Fat 2.26g	11%
Cholesterol 0.00mg	0%
Sodium 47.00mg	1%
Potassium 230.29mg	6%
Carbohydrates 3.85g	4%
Dietary Fiber 1.11g	4%
Protein 9.43g	18%
Iron 4.26mg	25%
Phosphorus 333.53mg	33%
Magnesium 151.82mg	37%

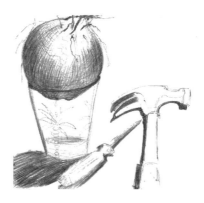

DESSERTS

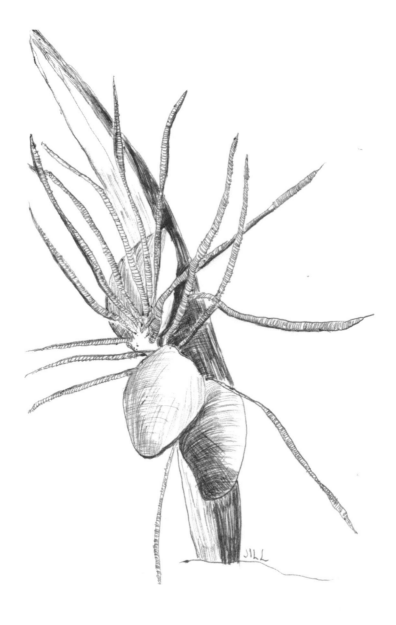

DESSERTS

CocoBerry Couscous Cake

serves 8

This cake is so easy to make and can be adapted to any fruit of the season.

Couscous Cake

2 1/2 cups	coconut water, or spring water
1 cup	couscous
	juice of 1/2 lemon
	dusting of extract
pinch	sea salt

Berry Topping

1 1/2 cups	blueberries, fresh or frozen
1 cup	coconut water or coconut milk
4 to 5 tsp.	agar agar flakes (kanten)
3 TB	coconut flakes
4 or more drops	stevia clear liquid or a dusting of extract
pinch	sea salt

Cake

1 Bring water to a boil in a saucepan. Stir in couscous, lemon, and stevia. Turn heat to low and simmer for about 5 minutes. Rinse a 9" spring form pan or shallow non-aluminum baking dish and spread the couscous firmly into it. Allow to set about 1 hour.

Nutrition Facts – 1 Serving	
Calories 153.64 **% Daily Value**	
Total Fat 1.25g	1%
Saturated Fat 0.96g	4%
Cholesterol 0.00mg	0%
Sodium 115.93mg	4%
Potassium 366.02mg	10%
Carbohydrates 32.84g	10%
Dietary Fiber 3.57g	14%
Protein 3.94g	7%

Berry Kanten Topping
1   Bring all ingredients to a boil, except coconut flakes. Lower heat and simmer for 8-10 minutes. Stir in the coconut flakes.
2   Set aside at room temperature until the kanten sauce begins to set, about 20 minutes. Spread it evenly over the cake. Sprinkle coconut flakes on top, if desired.
3   Refrigerate until set, about 1 hour.

Cooking Tips
The couscous can be prepared with Stevia GingerLemonade (pg. 28) instead of coconut water or spring water.

Baked Apple
serves 1

Apples that look old and wilting can produce a better taste than the designer ones. Choose the smallest and reddest apples.

apples
mixture of   coconut spread, sesame tahini, raisins, cinnamon, sea salt

1   Remove the core from the apple. Carefully remove the seeds without piercing the bottom.
2   Fill each apple with the mixture. Bake in 350 degree F. oven for 30 to 40 minutes.

Nutrition Facts – 1 Serving	
Calories 166.92 **% Daily Value**	
Total Fat 7.70g	11%
Saturated Fat 1.09g	5%
Cholesterol 0.00mg	0%
Sodium 11.10mg	0%
Potassium 220.80mg	6%
Carbohydrates 24.97g	8%
Dietary Fiber 5.12g	20%
Protein 2.93g	5%

Basic Pie Crust
serves 6/ yields 1 pie crust

The secret to successful pie dough is using ice-cold liquid and refrigerating the dough before rolling it. The more oil you add the flakier the crust.

1 cup	whole wheat flour or whole wheat pastry flour
1 cup	unbleached white flour or whole wheat flour
1/4 cup	coconut oil
1/4 tsp.	sea salt
4 or more TB	cold Stevia GingerLemonade (pg. 28) or spring water

1 Mix the flours and salt together in a large bowl. Mix in the oil with your hands until the dough forms a ball.

2 Add the ice-cold liquid and knead until the dough is smooth. Knead for a brief time, about 1 to 2 minutes. Place in the refrigerator for 30 minutes.

Nutrition Facts – 1 Serving	
Calories 223.93	**% Daily Value**
Total Fat 9.66g	14%
Saturated Fat 1.25g	6%
Cholesterol 0.00mg	0%
Sodium 79.75mg	3%
Potassium 103.29mg	2%
Carbohydrates 30.41g	10%
Dietary Fiber 3.00g	12%
Protein 4.89g	9%

3 Divide dough into 2 equal parts. Flour the surface you're using and the rolling pin. Make a ball with the dough and flatten with your palm. Roll out from the middle of the dough to the edge, moving in a circle until it's even and it's the thickness you want.

4 Oil and flour a pie pan. Trim off any excess dough and make a few pricks with a fork. Pre-bake for 10 minutes at 375 degrees F.

Barley Pudding
With PearGinger Sauce
serves 5

This is my signature dessert.

Barley Pudding

3 cups	spring water
1 cup	pearl barley
1 to 1 1/2 cups	coconut milk
5 to 10 drops	stevia clear liquid (to taste)
pinch	sea salt
1/4 tsp.	cinnamon

1   Wash the barley, add the spring water and soak overnight for best results. Bring soaking water and barley to a boil, lower heat and cook until water is absorbed, about 30 minutes.

2   When the barley has cooled, combine with other ingredients in a food processor and blend until smooth. Add more coconut milk for a creamier consistency.

3   Add PearGinger Sauce (pg. 133) on top of each serving and garnish with a mint leaf.

Nutrition Facts – 1 Serving

Calories 96.06	% Daily Value
Total Fat	
Saturated Fat 0.14g	0%
Cholesterol 0.00mg	0%
Sodium 12.51mg	0%
Potassium 130.42mg	3%
Carbohydrates 20.33g	6%
Dietary Fiber 1.83g	7%
Protein 2.06g	4%

Cooking Tips
When cooking barley as a grain, use 2 parts spring water to one part barley. For pudding, use 3 times spring water.
For rice pudding, substitute barley with a combination of short grain brown rice and sweet brown rice.

PearGinger Sauce
serves 4/yields 1 1/2 cups

Spoon this over puddings, muffins, couscous cake, pan-cakes, or enjoy as is.

2	pears, sliced
1 cup	Stevia GingerLemonade
pinch	sea salt
3 TB	arrowroot, dissolved in 4 TB GingerLemonade (pg. 29)

1   Place pears, salt and liquid in a saucepan. Bring to a boil, lower heat and simmer for 5 minutes or until pears are soft.
2   Purée in a blender.
3   Return to the saucepan, add the arrowroot mixture and slowly bring to a boil, stirring constantly. Once thickening occurs, stop stirring so as not to break down the bond and thin the sauce.

Nutrition Facts – 1 Serving	
Calories 0 **% Daily Value**	
Total Fat 0.00g	0%
Saturated Fat 0.00g	0%
Cholesterol 0.00mg	0%
Sodium 2.00mg	0%
Potassium 3.75mg	0%
Carbohydrates 0.11g	0%
Dietary Fiber 0.01g	0%
Protein 0.03g	0%

Chestnut Creme
serves 4/yields 2 cups

This can be served with toasted chopped almonds or hazelnuts on top, or used as pie filling.

2 cups	dried chestnuts or 1 lb. fresh chestnuts
	coconut milk to blend
	sea salt to taste
	cinnamon and nutmeg (optional)

Dried Chestnuts

1   Soak overnight in double spring water. Drain. Cook in a pot with double spring water and a pinch of sea salt until soft, approximately 20 to 25 minutes.
2   Remove to a chopping board and roughly chop. Purée in blender or food processor with just enough coconut milk to achieve a smooth consistency. Add spices if desired.

Nutrition Facts – 1 Serving	
Calories 323.13	**% Daily Value**
Total Fat 5.86g	9%
Saturated Fat 4.17g	20%
Cholesterol 0.00mg	0%
Sodium 77.06mg	3%
Potassium 608.06mg	17%
Carbohydrates 62.38g	20%
Dietary Fiber 0.41g	1%
Protein 5.68g	11%
Vitamin C 45.53mg	75%
Vitamin B6 0.52mg	25%
Magnesium 105.62mg	27%

Fresh Chestnuts

1   Remove the shells and cook in boiling spring water for ten minutes. Skim them out - the brown skin should come off easily. Place them back in the boiling water and cook until tender when pierced with a fork.
2   Prepare as above.

Coconut Date Cake

serves 6 to 8

This recipe makes two layers or one large (10-inch x 14-inch) cake.

Liquid Ingredients

2 cups	coconut milk
1 1/2 cups	dates, pitted
1/2 cup	coconut oil
1	orange, extract the juice and grate the rind

Dry Ingredients

1 cup	unbleached flour, sifted
2 cups	whole wheat pastry flour, sifted
1 TB	non-aluminum baking powder
pinch	sea salt
1/2 cup	coconut flakes

1   Combine coconut milk and dates in a saucepan. Simmer until dates are very soft. Place dates and coconut mixture in a blender; add oil, grated orange rind and juice and purée until smooth.

2   Combine dry ingredients into a bowl. Pour liquid ingredients into dry and mix until well coated. The batter will be thick.

3   Spoon batter into oiled baking dish. Bake at 350 degrees F. for 35 to 45 minutes, until firm and golden.

4   Spread cake with coconut spread, or garnish with coconut flakes, chopped walnuts or almonds.

Nutrition Facts – 1 Serving	
Calories 580.45	**% Daily Value**
Total Fat 35.82g	55%
Saturated Fat 30.79g	153%
Cholesterol 0.00mg	0%
Sodium 15.93mg	0%
Potassium 592.50mg	14%
Carbohydrates 64.94g	21%
Dietary Fiber 9.18g	36%
Protein 8.68g	17%
Iron 4.87mg	27%

Cocoa Almond Pudding
serves 3/yields 1 1/2 cups

This makes a delicious pie filling for Pie Crust in the Raw or Basic Pie Crust, or layered with fruit for fruit parfait, or served frozen as almond sorbet.

6 oz.	coconut cream
1 cup	coconut milk
2 to 3 TB.	almond butter
4 large	Medjool dates, pits removed and chopped
2 TB	unroasted cocoa powder
1 tsp.	vanilla extract
pinch	sea salt
	stevia clear liquid to taste

Nutrition Facts – 1 Serving	
Calories 453.39 **% Daily Value**	
Total Fat 43.72g	67%
Saturated Fat 33.61g	168%
Cholesterol 0.00mg	0%
Sodium 14.50mg	0%
Potassium 568.61mg	16%
Carbohydrates 18.66g	6%
Dietary Fiber 3.74g	14%
Protein 6.23g	12%
Iron 4.88mg	27%
Magnesium 105.62mg	26%

1   Blend all ingredients in a food processor until creamy. Adjust sweetness to taste.

Date Nut Treat

A treat for one.

1	Medjool date, pitted
2 TB	coconut cream
2 or 3	walnut halves, finely chopped
	coconut flakes

Nutrition Facts – 1 Serving	
Calories 580.45 **% Daily Value**	
Total Fat 35.82g	55%
Saturated Fat 30.79g	153%
Cholesterol 0.00mg	0%
Sodium 15.93mg	0%
Potassium 592.50mg	14%
Carbohydrates 64.94g	21%
Dietary Fiber 9.18g	36%
Protein 8.68g	17%

1   Dice the date and combine with chopped walnuts. Blend in the coconut cream.
2   Form into 1 or 2 firm balls and roll in coconut flakes. Refrigerate.

Crème de Plantain
serves 2

This dessert is sinfully simple. Choose a plantain that is very ripe with a black skin. Just a touch of garlic enlivens this banana-like smoothie.

Crème

1 ripe	plantain, sliced
1/4 clove	garlic, minced
1/4 cup	lime juice
1 TB	coconut cream
few drops	stevia clear liquid
pinch	sea salt
	coconut flakes for garnish

Crust Ingredients

4 TB	golden flax seeds, ground in a coffee grinder or blender
4 TB	lime juice
2 to 4 drops	stevia clear liquid or to taste

1   Place all Crème ingredients, except coconut flakes, in a blender and blend until smooth. Add more lime juice if needed to blend ingredients. Adjust sweetness to taste.

2   Crust: Mix the stevia and lime juice together in a cup. Add to the ground flax seeds and blend. Place on the bottom of a parfait dish and cover with the plantain mixture. Garnish with coconut flakes.

Nutrition Facts – 1 Serving	
Calories 269.28 **% Daily Value**	
Total Fat 11.16g	17%
Saturated Fat 3.21g	16%
Cholesterol 0.00mg	0%
Sodium 12.73mg	0%
Potassium 703.21mg	20%
Carbohydrates 42.95g	14%
Dietary Fiber 9.17g	36%
Protein 6.41g	12%
Vitamin C 35.15mg	47%

Sumptuous Carob Cream

This is very rich and very delicious.

1/2 cup	coconut cream
1 to 2 TB	roasted carob powder
1 TB	coconut flakes
pinch	ground cloves
	stevia clear liquid, extract powder, or concentrate to taste

1 In a small bowl, combine all ingredients and blend. Adjust seasonings and sweetness to taste.

Nutrition Facts – 1 Serving	
Calories 458.82 **% Daily Value**	
Total Fat 46.86g	72%
Saturated Fat 41.52g	207%
Cholesterol 0.00mg	0%
Sodium 7.50mg	0%
Potassium 488.37mg	13%
Carbohydrates 14.31g	4%
Dietary Fiber 5.36g	21%
Protein 5.18g	10%

Pie Crust In The Raw
serves 6/yields 1 pie crust

1/2 lb.	combination of dried fruits such as: coconut flakes, figs, pineapple, papaya, mango, and fresh Medjool dates
1/4 cup	finely chopped walnuts, almonds, or hazelnuts

Nutrition Facts – 1 Serving	
Calories 124.55 **% Daily Value**	
Total Fat 3.45g	5%
Saturated Fat 0.32g	1%
Cholesterol 0.00mg	0%
Sodium 6.90mg	0%
Potassium 322.94mg	9%
Carbohydrates 24.90g	8%
Dietary Fiber 3.28g	13%
Protein 1.69g	3%

1 Blend dried fruit in a food processor on the S blade. Press into a pie plate. Top with the chopped nuts.

Mango Creamsickle
serves 2/yields 2 cups

This reminds me of the creamsickles I used to buy as a child from the ice cream man as he drove through our neighborhood playing his happy tunes.

2 cups	fresh mango pulp
2 TB or more	coconut milk
	stevia clear liquid - to taste, if needed

1   Purée mango pulp and coconut milk in a blender or food processor.
2   Place mixture in ice cube trays and freeze.
3   Remove frozen mango cubes and place in a blender or food processor. Add enough coconut milk to blend the mixture and pulse until creamy. If needed, add stevia clear liquid to taste after blending.
4   Enjoy immediately.

Cooking Tips
If fresh mangos aren't available, use packaged frozen mango slices. Defrost before using.

Nutrition Facts – 1 Serving	
Calories 117.35 **% Daily Value**	
Total Fat 1.03g	1%
Saturated Fat 0.17g	0%
Cholesterol 0.00mg	0%
Sodium 6.97mg	0%
Potassium 300.55mg	8%
Carbohydrates 28.60g	9%
Dietary Fiber 3.37g	13%
Protein 1.68g	3%
Vitamin A 6434.89IU	47%
Vitamin C 45.71mg	76%

Lemon Cookies
with Coconut Lime Sauce

serves 18/yields 1 1/2

YUM!

Dry Ingredients

1 cup	whole wheat pastry flour
1 cup	oat flakes, ground in a blender or coffee mill
1/2 cup	golden flax seeds, ground in a coffee mill or blender
1/2 tsp.	stevia extract
1/2 tsp.	cinnamon

Liquid Ingredients

3/4 cup	coconut milk
1/4 cup	sesame tahini
1/3 cup	soft tofu
1 tsp.	vanilla extract
1 tsp.	grated lemon rind
1/2 tsp.	stevia clear liquid

Coconut Lime Sauce - blend all in a bowl

1/3 cup	coconut milk
2 TB	coconut spread
2 to 3 TB	lime juice - to your taste
	finely grated peel of 1 lime
several drops	stevia clear liquid or dusting of extract powder - to your taste
few pinches	cinnamon

1 Preheat oven to 350 degrees.
2 Blend the dry ingredients together in a bowl.
3 In a separate bowl, blend liquid ingredients. Fold in dry ingredients and gently blend.
4 Lightly oil 2 cookie sheets. Use about 2 TB batter for each cookie, form into balls and gently flatten. (Moisten hands if batter is too sticky). Bake for 20 to 30 minutes. Cool before serving.
5 Spoon sauce over each cookie.

Nutrition Facts – 1 Serving	
Calories 118.91 **% Daily Value**	
Total Fat 7.58g	11%
Saturated Fat 3.93g	19%
Cholesterol 12.00mg	4%
Sodium 7.82mg	0%
Potassium 129.36mg	3%
Carbohydrates 10.67g	3%
Dietary Fiber 3.01g	12%
Protein 3.68g	7%

Cooking Tips
The ginger grater achieves the best results for grating lime peel.

Tapioca Pudding
serves 2

Tapioca, or sago, is made from the root of the cassava plant. I learned about this special pudding from fellow students at a Temple Training I attended in the mountains of Japan. They had been obsessing about it throughout the whole 2 months. After the training, we traveled by Orient Express to Penang, Malaysia, then ferried over to Batu Ferringhi, home of this famous Sago Café. It was love at first bite. Here's a healthier version without the sugar.

1/4 cup	small tapioca pearls
1 cup	coconut milk
1 cup	spring water
few pinches	ground cloves
	pinch of sea salt
	dusting of stevia extract or the clear liquid to taste
	coconut flakes for garnish

1   Combine coconut milk, water, tapioca, salt, and cloves in a saucepan. Bring to a slow boil, turn heat to low, stirring frequently to prevent the bottom from sticking.
2   Cook for about 20 minutes or longer until there are no more white balls and the tapioca is nearly clear. Add stevia.
3   Place in individual bowls and chill.
4   To serve, drizzle on coconut milk or coconut cream and garnish with coconut flakes.

Nutrition Facts – 1 Serving

Calories 317.20	**% Daily Value**
Total Fat 28.68g	44%
Saturated Fat 25.39g	126%
Cholesterol 0.00mg	0%
Sodium 162.60mg	6%
Potassium 385.38mg	11%
Carbohydrates 16.45g	5%
Dietary Fiber 3.10g	12%
Protein 3.10g	6%

Cooking Tips
The proportion is about 6 times liquid to 1 part tapioca. Longer cooking will result in a thicker consistency. It also thickens when it cools. If it's too thick, add more liquid.

Peach Pie in Coconut Crème Sauce

serves 4

This tropical dessert is appropriate for a summer day. The piecrust makes this dessert so sweet, four people can eat it twice.

Peaches and Crème

3 to 4	peaches sliced, skin on
	juice of 1 lime
1 tsp.	ginger juice
	pinch of sea salt
1 cup	coconut milk, diluted with 1/3 cup spring water
3 to 6 drops	stevia clear liquid
pinch	ground cloves or nutmeg
2 to 2 1/2 TB	arrowroot dissolved in 3 TB spring water or coconut water

Pie Crust in the Raw (pg. 138)

1   In a saucepan, combine all ingredients except arrowroot mixture. Slowly bring to a boil, stirring constantly. Simmer for about 5 minutes, until the peaches are soft.

2   Add the arrowroot mixture and stir constantly for a few minutes, until it begins to thicken. Allow to cool, then spread over Pie Crust in the Raw.

Nutrition Facts – 1 Serving

Calories 125.07	% Daily Value
Total Fat 8.12g	12%
Saturated Fat 7.14g	35%
Cholesterol 0.00mg	0%
Sodium 75.48mg	3%
Potassium 250.80mg	7%
Carbohydrates 14.02g	4%
Dietary Fiber 1.84g	7%
Protein 1.37g	2%

Cooking Tips

Any of the following summer fruits can be substituted for peaches: nectarines, bananas, apricots, mangos or papayas.

Pumpkin Pie
serves 6/yields 1 9-inch pie

The Japanese Hokkaido pumpkin or buttercup squash work well for this recipe. Naturally, the success of this pie depends on how sweet the pumpkin is. The pulp should be a bright orange color. If it's not sweet, you'll need to sweeten the mixture with any form of stevia.

1 medium	pumpkin or squash
2 TB	coconut spread
about 1 cup	Stevia GingerLemonade (pg. 28)
2 TB	sesame tahini
pinch each	nutmeg, cinnamon, sea salt

1   Peel and clean the inside of the pumpkin. Cut into small cubes and place in a pot with almost enough Stevia GingerLemonade to cover. Cover and cook until soft. If there is still liquid remaining, remove the cover and boil off the liquid.

2   Purée the pumpkin in a blender or food processor with the rest of the ingredients. Adjust sweetness to taste.

3   Pour filling in a prebaked piecrust and bake at 350 F. degrees for 15 to 25 minutes.

Nutrition Facts – 1 Serving

Calories 62.12	**% Daily Value**	
Total Fat 3.66g		5%
Saturated Fat 1.36g		6%
Cholesterol 0.00mg		0%
Sodium 9.19mg		0%
Potassium 230.10mg		6%
Carbohydrates 6.94g		2%
Dietary Fiber 1.47g		5%
Protein 1.90g		3%
Vitamin A 2358.15IU		47%

Sticky Black Rice

serves 4

Black rice (a.k.a. purple rice) is indigenous to South East Asia. It is sweet with a glutinous texture and prepared as a dessert. Typically, it is steamed in a banana leaf with bananas, coconut and palm sugar.

1 cup	black rice
3 cups	spring water
1 or more	bananas, sliced thin
pinch	sea salt
	coconut milk or coconut cream
to taste	stevia clear liquid or a dusting of extract

1   Rinse rice until water clears. Cover with at least 2" spring water and soak 4 or more hours.

2   Bring rice, water and sea salt to a boil in a saucepan. Lower heat and simmer for about 40 to 50 minutes, until liquid is absorbed.

3   At this point, you can add 2 or more bananas and blend in while it's still hot; or remove from the heat, allow to cool and add the banana slices to each individual bowl. Add your choice and amount of stevia and top with coconut milk or coconut cream.

4   Serve warm, room temperature or chilled.

Nutrition Facts – 1 Serving	
Calories 224.63	**% Daily Value**
Total Fat 4.58g	7%
Saturated Fat 3.14g	15%
Cholesterol 0.00mg	0%
Sodium 9.09mg	0%
Potassium 283.18mg	8%
Carbohydrates 42.77g	14%
Dietary Fiber 3.45g	13%
Protein 4.05g	8%

Cooking Tips
This rice is available at Asian markets.

Quinoa Custard

serves 4

1 cup	quinoa, rinsed well through a strainer to remove its bitter surface.
2 cups	spring water
pinch	sea salt
2 TB	almond butter
1 cup	coconut milk
to taste	stevia clear liquid or dusting of extract

1   Place rinsed quinoa, water and sea salt in a saucepan. Cover and bring to a boil, reduce heat to low and simmer until liquid is absorbed, about 15 minutes. Remove to a bowl, fluff with chopsticks or a fork and allow to cool.

2   Combine quinoa with the rest of the ingredients in a blender or food processor and blend until smooth. Add more liquid for a creamier consistency. Adjust sweetness to taste.

Nutrition Facts – 1 Serving

Calories 219.70	**% Daily Value**	
Total Fat 7.78g	11%	
Saturated Fat 0.76g	3%	
Cholesterol 0.00mg	0%	
Sodium 17.03mg	0%	
Potassium 418.32mg	11%	
Carbohydrates 31.53g	10%	
Dietary Fiber 3.20g	12%	
Protein 7.62g	15%	
Iron 4.42mg	25%	
Magnesium 120.49mg	30%	

Millet Mousse

If you have leftover millet, this simple dessert will be ready in minutes. It can be prepared with bananas or any ripe fruit, and warming spices such as allspice, cinnamon, nutmeg, cloves, or ginger.

1 cup	cooked millet
1/2 cup	coconut milk
1/4 tsp.	ground cloves
	stevia extract or clear liquid to taste
	coconut cream, coconut flakes and cinnamon

1   Purée all ingredients in a food processor or blender. Add more or less of the coconut milk depending on your desired consistency.

2   On each serving, dust with cinnamon, sprinkle with coconut flakes and drizzle on coconut cream.

Nutrition Facts – 1 Serving

	% Daily Value
Calories 218.08	
Total Fat 16.22g	24%
Saturated Fat 13.95g	69%
Cholesterol 0.00mg	0%
Sodium 3.38mg	0%
Potassium 184.14mg	5%
Carbohydrates 16.83g	5%
Dietary Fiber 1.80g	7%
Protein 3.68g	7%

Cooking Tips

To cook millet, combine 1 part well rinsed millet to 3 parts spring water in a pot. Cover and bring to a boil. Reduce heat to low and cook until all the water is absorbed, about 45 minutes.

Glossary of Ingredients

AGAR-AGAR (also called kanten) is a variety of red sea vegetables used as a substitute for gelatin (an animal product). It is used with fruit juice to make jello, for aspics, custards, and to thicken puddings and sauces. It is rich in calcium, iron, and natural iodine. It promotes digestion and is useful to dieters. It comes in 3 forms: a bar, flakes, and powder. One bar gels 2 cups of liquid and equals 1/4 tsp. of the powder or 3 to 4 TB. of the flakes.

ALMOND BUTTER is similar to peanut butter, but made from almonds. Available raw or roasted.

ARROWROOT FLOUR comes from the arrowroot plant. It will thicken cooking liquids or stews and is a healthy substitute for cornstarch. Dilute in an equal amount of room temperature spring water.

AMARANTH is an ancient Aztec grain. Its tiny kernels are high in protein and lysine and contain 60-mg. calcium per half a cup. It is gluten free with a nutty taste and a glutinous texture. It becomes rancid quickly, so refrigerate. Combines well with quinoa, millet and buckwheat.

CAROB FLOUR is a pod from a Mediterranean tree. It is caffeine-free with alkalizing properties and is used as a substitute for chocolate. Carob flour is similar to cocoa although sweeter, lower in fat and rich in iron, Vitamin B6, calcium and other minerals. It is available as roasted or unroasted.

COCONUT BUTTER and coconut oil are essentially the same. In northern countries this oil remains in a solid state most of the year and is referred to as coconut butter. In warmer countries (where they are produced) they remain in a liquid state.

COUSCOUS is a traditional Near-Eastern food. The refined variety is made from pre-cooked, coarsely ground semolina wheat. The whole wheat variety is made from whole Durham wheat and is more nutritious.

FLAX SEEDS are small seeds rich in essential fatty acids. Although both the brown and golden varieties have the same nutritional value, the golden variety has a more delicate texture and grinds to a finer consistency.

GREEN ONIONS are also called scallions.

MILLET is a tiny, golden grain that is widely used in China, India and Europe. It is the most alkaline of all grains and is safe for those with wheat intolerance.

MISO is a fermented paste made from beans (mainly soybeans), grains and salt. It is high in protein and amino acids. The darker the miso is, the longer the fermenting process. Because it is a live food, it should not be boiled, but rather added at the end of the cooking process and allowed to simmer for a few minutes. Choose miso that is unpasteurized, aged, GMO free, and contains sea salt.

MUNG BEANS, a member of the kidney bean family, are small, sweet green beans popular in the Near East and in India. It is best known as sprouted mung beans, which are eaten as a fresh vegetable or in stir-fry dishes. Dried mung beans are delicious simmered with spices and served as a thick sauce spooned over grains. It is an alkaline food and is beneficial to the liver and gall bladder.

QUINOA (keen'wa), an ancient Incan grain, is actually the fruit of a plant. Like amaranth, it is high in protein and lysine. It contains more iron, phosphorus, vitamins A, E and B, and more calcium and fat than other grains. Its protective coating, saponin, has a bitter taste and must be rinsed off under cold water before cooking. It quadruples in size when cooked. Combines well with millet, amaranth and buckwheat.

SEA VEGETABLES (seaweed) include arame, hijiki, dulse, wakame, nori, kelp, kombu and alaria. All are rich in essential minerals and vitamins and are especially beneficial to the thyroid and for weight loss.

SESAME SEEDS are high in calcium, iron and phosphorus as well as essential fatty acids. Black seeds have a stronger flavor.

SESAME TAHINI is similar to peanut butter, but made from ground sesame seeds. Available raw and roasted.

SHOYU is a soy sauce made from fermented soybeans, wheat and sea salt. Add it as a seasoning at the end of the cooking process as not to diminish its delicate flavor.

TAMARI is a wheat free soy sauce made as a byproduct of miso. It contains soy, sea salt and spring water. It is high in amino acids and has a stronger flavor than shoyu. It can be cooked longer with foods without losing flavor. It is not to be used to season food at the table.

TAPIOCA or sago, is made from the root of the cassava or yucca plant, native to South America and the West Indies.

TEMPEH is a fermented food made from soybeans. It is rich in protein and B vitamins. Its strong taste makes it a popular substitute for meat.

TOFU is made from cooked soybeans and nigari, a natural solidifier. Poor quality tofu uses a chemical nigari or alum as the solidifying agent. Tofu is high in protein, B vitamins and minerals and it is reported to be effective in hormone replacement therapy. It is available in extra firm, firm, soft or silken depending on how much water is extracted during the production. Choose non-GMO.

UMEBOSHI PLUMS are a traditional Japanese food. These salted, sour plums are prepared through a long fermenting stage and are used to balance and preserve food. They are reputed to be the most alkalizing food on earth. The whole plums and plum paste are suitable for cooking. For strictly medicinal purposes, it is available as a concentrated paste or in tiny balls. (I never travel without it.)

UMEBOSHI VINEGAR is the by-product left over from the pickling liquid of the umeboshi plums.

WHOLE GRAIN RICE: Brown rice is available as short grain (nutty, chewy and best eaten in colder weather), medium grain (good for all climates), long grain (lighter, fluffier and best in warm weather), basmati (aromatic, lighter than long grain and best in warm weather) and sweet or glutinous (contains more protein and fat than other rice and best cooked with other grains or beans). Wehani is a long grain red rice, chewy, sweet and similar to basmati. Black rice is a glutinous, sweet, whole grain variety indigenous to South East Asia.

WILD RICE is not a true rice but more closely related to corn; native to the Great Lakes region. It is still harvested by Native Americans. This slim, dark brown grain has an exquisite nutty flavor. It has more protein than other rice and is rich in minerals and B vitamins. Because of its diuretic effect, it is known to benefit the kidneys and bladder. Since it is expensive, it is commonly combined with other grains. For example, add 1/4 cup wild rice to 1 cup brown rice.

STEVIA

Recommended Products

These are my recommendations of companies who maintain high standards and integrity and a dedication to providing best quality products. If your local store does not carry their products, you may want to ask the store manager about distributing products from these companies, or you may contact the companies directly.

Wilderness Family Naturals – organic, unrefined coconut oil, coconut water, coconut milk, coconut cream, coconut spread, coconut flakes and tools; www.wildernessfamilynaturals.com; (800) 945-3801
Nutiva – organic, unrefined coconut oil; www.nutiva.com; (800) 993-43
Jungle Products – organic, unrefined coconut and red palm oils; www.junglepi.com; (707) 433-8777

SweetLeaf Stevia – stevia tea bags, extract, clear liquid, SteviaPlus, concentrate, individual packets; www.sweetleaf.com; (800) 899-9908

JBB Stevia Laboratories – Japanese producers of stevia fertilizer for agriculture, fisheries and livestock; www.jbb-stevia.com

Mountain Valley Growers – organically grown stevia plants and herbs; www.mountainvalleygrowers.com; (559) 338-2775

The Grain and Salt Society – Celtic sea salt, macrobiotic foods, kitchenware, body care; www.celtic-seasalt.com; (800) 867-7258

Natural Import Co. – mail order for Japanese ginger grater and other kitchenware, and a full line of macrobiotic foods; www.qualitynaturalfoods.com; (800) 324-1878

Azure Standard – supplier of 6,000 organic natural foods and products; www.azurestandard.com; (541) 467-2230

Arrowhead Mills – flour products and dry mixes; www.arrowheadmills.com; (800) 434-4246

Bob's Red Mill Natural Foods – millers of natural whole grain flours, cereals and baking mixes; www.bobsredmill.com; (800) 553-2258

GoldMine Natural Food Co. – mail order for organic/macrobiotic foods, kitchenware, body care; www.goldminenaturalfood.com; (800) 475-FOOD

Glaser Organic Farms – mail order for organic/ wild harvested produce, nut butters, raw prepared foods; www.glaserorganicfarms.com; (305) 238-7747

SunOrganic Farm – mail order for organic dried fruits, nuts, nut butters, herbs/seasonings; www.sunorganic.com; (800) 269-9888

Eden Foods – organic manufacturer of packaged foods and importer of Japanese macrobiotic foods; www.edenfoods.com; (888) 441-3336

Southern Brown Rice – growers of high quality organic brown and wild rice; www.southernbrownrice.com; (800) 421-7423

Diamond Organics – mail order for organic produce and groceries; www.diamondorganics.com; (888) ORGANIC

Maine Seaweed – hand harvested Maine seaweed; www.maineseaweedcompany.com; (207) 546-2875

RocaMojo – organic coffee substitutes: ground roasted soybeans and a blend of coffee and roasted soybeans; www.rocamojo.com; (818) 961-0484

Frontier and Simply Organic – organic herbs and spices; www.frontiercoop.com; (850) 656-6548

French Meadow Bakery – organic yeast-free breads; www.frenchmeadow.com; (612) 870-4740

Kitchen's Best Manufacturing – Soyquick Automatic Soymilk Maker; www.soymilkquick.com; (888) 769-5433

Zojirushi America Corp. – Japanese manufacturer of rice cookers and other kitchen appliances; www.zojirushi.com; (800) 733-6270

Index

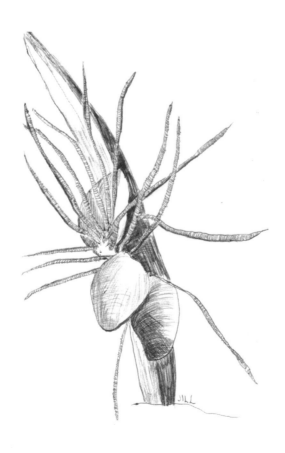

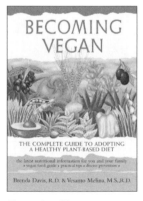